CREEPY *and* TRUE

GHOSTS UNVEILED!

KERRIE LOGAN HOLLIHAN

ABRAMS BOOKS FOR YOUNG READERS

NEW YORK

To my sister Anne Logan German,

who shall forever be "Tinker"

Front cover: Built in 1893, the Littlefield House in
Austin, Texas, is no stranger to ghosts. There have been ghost sightings,
unexplained bumps in the night, and items moved from place to place.

Cataloging-in-Publication Data has been applied for and
may be obtained from the Library of Congress.

ISBN 978-1-4197-4679-6

Text copyright © 2020 Kerrie Logan Hollihan
Edited by Howard W. Reeves
Book design by Becky James

For picture credits, see page 191.

Printed and bound in China
10 9 8 7 6 5 4 3 2

Abrams Books for Young Readers are available at special discounts when
purchased in quantity for premiums and promotions as well as fundraising or
educational use. Special editions can also be created to specification. For details,
contact specialsales@abramsbooks.com or the address below.

Abrams® is a registered trademark of Harry N. Abrams, Inc.

ABRAMS The Art of Books
195 Broadway, New York, NY 10007
abramsbooks.com

CONTENTS

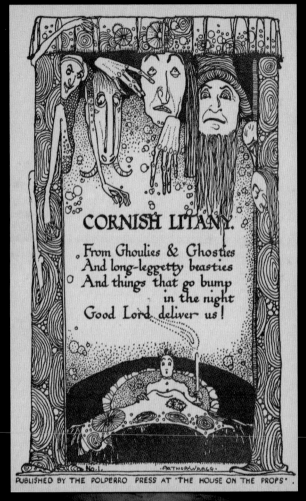

CORNISH LITANY.

From Ghoulies & Ghosties
And long-leggetty beasties
And things that go bump
        in the night
Good Lord, deliver us!

No. 1.   ARTHUR WRAGG.

PUBLISHED BY THE POLPERRO PRESS AT "THE HOUSE ON THE PROPS".

Artist Arthur Wragg illustrated the Cornish Litany
in the early 1920s.

INTRODUCTION

From ghoulies & ghosties and
long-leggetty beasties
And things that go bump in the night
Good Lord, deliver us!
—An old Cornish prayer

I ain't afraid of no ghosts!
—*Ghostbusters*

Do you believe in ghosts? Agreed, ghosts are creepy.

Tune in to any number of cable channels or podcasts, and you'll discover people armed with every kind of electronic gadget searching for ghosts or ghouls or things that go bump in the night. There are well-documented accounts of ghost sightings, and many very reliable folks—like ministers, school principals, teachers, and others—supply them.

Or you might be the ghost-disbelieving kind. Lots of people think the notion of ghosts is just plain silly. They think that ghosts can all be explained by science.

Some scientists believe that seeing ghosts is simply a symptom of the brain not doing its job. Brain damage, illness, or even waking up sleep-deprived and groggy can make us "see things" that are not real. You can read about this in all kinds of science journals and magazines.

But, as the pages that follow will reveal, there are lots of ghosts to chase down—all around the globe. Not ghost stories, which we have aplenty, but sightings of ghosts that are based in truth, in actual events. For the people who see them, ghosts are true. Very true. The Pew Research Center, a big-time group that asks ordinary people what they think, declared in October 2015, "Nearly one-in-five U.S. adults (18%) say they've seen or been in the presence of a ghost."

In the spirit of researching this book, I reached out to people I encounter every day to ask, "Do you believe in ghosts?" I first started with Tia, a sixth grader who lived across the street from me and was hanging with her friend.

"Do you believe in ghosts?" I asked. "No," Tia said without hesitation.

Her friend answered by screwing up her face and saying, "Maybeeeeee."

Then almost in unison the girls exclaimed, "But there's a girl in our class, and she talks to them all the time!"

There you have it. To the people who see them, ghosts are quite true.

When I was thirteen years old, in 1965, my grandmother died. We lived near Chicago, and our family took a passenger train overnight to northwestern North Dakota, where Grandma was to be buried. It was a very sad time for our family, especially for my little sister, Anne, who was ten.

She was Grandma's "favorite," I think; they had a very close relationship for the few years that Grandma lived near our home. Anne would stop by every day after school to say hello. Grandma loved all her grandchildren, of course, but she and Anne shared an extra bit of special understanding.

"Grandma didn't smile much for pictures," the author recalls. The author, her grandmother Bertha Johnson, and her sister, Anne.

After we returned home from Grandma's funeral, our mom had a visitor stop by. I heard Mama tell her friend how sad Anne had been about Grandma's death. Mama had noticed how my sister had lingered at the cemetery to watch from afar as Grandma's casket was lowered into the ground.

It wasn't until we were both grown up, with kids of our own, that Anne told me a secret. Not long after Grandma died, she had visited Anne in the middle of the night.

"She was patting my left lower leg. The covers were up, and she was sitting on the end of the bed," Anne remembered.

Anne says she woke up. She could feel Grandma's form as she sat there.

"I'm okay, Tinkie," Grandma said to her. "You don't need to worry about me." Tinkie was her pet name for my sister.

Anne is a straight-talking, sensible woman. To this day, she insists that Grandma's visit was real:

"Thinking back on my experience, I don't recall ever considering Grandma as a ghost or a spirit. She appeared as a live person, just her. I didn't think of the experience as being unusual at the time. It wasn't until I told others that the word *ghost* or *spirit* was used."

There's no end to what you can learn about ghosts. Let this book be your beginning.

Before we start, it might be helpful to learn a few synonyms for a ghost. There are *specters*, for instance, which make spectral appearances, and *apparitions* that appear. *Haunt* is a word used as both subject and verb, but *haint* might be new to you. (It's a ghost, BTW.)

If you are German, a ghost is *ein Geist,* and in Spain it's *un fantasma.* In French that would be *un fantôme.* Which ties back to English, right? Phantoms are ghosts, too. Words have family histories, just as people do!

One more vocabulary word you probably know but might not know why: Often when we watch shows or videos about ghosts, hosts of "paranormal investigators" are swarming around. They are armed with high-tech electronics to detect signs, sounds, or smells that indicate ghosts are present. *Paranormal* means not explainable scientifically. It first showed up in print in about 1905. *Para* has its roots in ancient Greek, meaning "by the side of, beside, by, past, or beyond." You already know what *normal* means.

BTW. As I edited this book and added this last paragraph, I couldn't get my keyboard to type quotation marks around "paranormal." I went back and tried to make that fix, and I could not. Weird!!!!

In 1888, a book entitled *Fairy and Folk Tales of the Irish Peasantry* describes a banshee as "an attendant fairy that follows the old families . . . and wails before a death." To this day, folks fear her animal-like howls and screams.

FACTLET

A GHOST BY ANY OTHER NAME . . .

IN THE NINETEENTH CENTURY, an author in England named Michael Aislabie Denham (1801–1859) collected many pieces of folklore—old stories that people, poor or rich, liked to tell. Many spoke of ghosts that haunted this or that building or piece of ground. In fact, any place in England that had a bit of history was likely to be haunted.

England's history reaches back thousands of years, so that's a gigantic number of spots open to ghosts. Denham claimed, "There was not a village in England that had not its own peculiar ghost."

HE SPELLED OUT EVERY NAME ONE HEARD THAT REFERRED TO GHOST AND FAIRY NAMES:

"Boggles, Bloody Bones, spirits, demons, ignis fatui, brownies, bugbears, black dogs, spectres, shellycoats, scarecrows, witches, wizards, barguests, Robin-Goodfellows, hags, night-bats, scrags, breaknecks, fantasms, hobgoblins, hobhoulards, boggy-boes, dobbies, hob-thrusts, fetches, kelpies, warlocks, mock-beggars, mum-pokers, Jemmy-burties, urchins, satyrs, pans, fauns, sirens, tritons, centaurs, calcars, nymphs, imps, incubuses, spoorns, men-in-the-oak, hell-wains, fire-drakes, kit-a-can-sticks, Tom-tumblers, melch-dicks, larrs, kitty-witches, hobby-lanthorns, Dick-a-Tuesdays, Elf-fires, Gyl-burnt-tales, knockers, elves, rawheads, Meg-with-the-wads, old-shocks, ouphs, pad-foots, pixies, pictrees, giants, dwarfs, Tom-pokers, tutgots, snapdragons, sprets, spunks, conjurers, thurses, spurns, tantarrabobs, swaithes, tints, tod-lowries, Jack-in-the-Wads, mormos, changelings, redcaps, yeth-hounds, colt-pixies, Tom-thumbs, black-bugs, boggarts, scar-bugs, shag-foals, hodge-pochers, hob-thrushes, bugs, bull-beggars, bygorns, bolls, caddies, bomen, brags, wraiths, waffs, flay-boggarts, fiends, gallytrots, imps, gytrashes, patches, hob-and-lanthorns, gringes, boguests, bonelesses, Peg-powlers, pucks, fays, kidnappers, gallybeggars, hudskins, nickers, madcaps, trolls, robinets, friars' lanthorns, silkies, cauld-lads, death-hearses, goblins, hob-headlesses, buga-boos, kows, or cowes, nickies, nacks, waiths, miffies, buckies, ghouls, sylphs, guests, swarths, freiths, freits, gy-carlins, pig-mies, chittifaces, nixies, Jinny-burnt-tails, dudmen, hell-hounds, dopple-gangers, boggleboes, bogies, portunes, grants, hobbits, hobgoblins, cowies, dunnies, wirrikows, al-holdes, mannikins, follets, korreds, lubberkins, cluri-cauns, kobolds, leprechauns, kors, mares, korreds, puckles korigans, sylvans, succubuses, shadows, banshees, lian-hanshees, clabbernappers, Gabriel-hounds, mawkins, doubles, corpse lights or candles, scrats, mahounds, trows, gnomes, sprites, fates, fiends, sibyls, nicknevins, fairies, thrummy-caps, cutties, and nisses . . ."

That would be 192 terms for *ghost*. Add *poltergeist*, a German word that showed up in English about 1850, and that's a grand total of 193!

CHAPTER ONE

THE DEATHLY DOMESTICATED–GHOST DOGS AND CATS

DOGS AND CATS ARE OUR CLOSEST ANIMAL FRIENDS. Humans domesticated dogs—invited them to live with us—at least fifteen thousand years ago and maybe much earlier.

Cats, on the other hand, independent as they are, seem to have chosen to live with us, according to recent science studies.

Either way, dogs and cats share our lives, beloved pets that we mourn when they die. What then? If loved ones appear as ghosts, why not cats and dogs, as well?

A CREEPY CANINE IN CONNECTICUT

The dog, aka man's best friend, has wagged a ghostly tale for hundreds of years, especially in the British Isles. Often these creepy companions appear as big black dogs with glowing red eyes. On the southeast coast of England, a hellhound named Black Shuck has raised the hair on the back of people's necks since 1577.

Black dogs haunt Americans, too. In the Hanging Hills near Meriden, Connecticut, hikers have met a small black pooch that seems friendly—at first. You don't want to meet him three times, however.

The pup's spine-chilling story appeared in 1898 in the *Connecticut Quarterly*, a magazine of nonfiction, poetry, and fiction. It was thick with words, and stories ran on for pages.

"The Black Dog" opened with a warning. Keep this in mind:

> And if a man shall meet the Black Dog once, it shall be for joy; and if twice, it shall be for sorrow; and the third time, he shall die.

The author of "The Black Dog" was a Harvard University graduate student named W. H. C. Pynchon. Pynchon studied geology, Earth's history as it was recorded in rocks. His story traced events that had befallen him ten years earlier in the Hanging Hills.

Pynchon had driven a horse and wagon up a quiet path to a high point called West Peak. As he drove upward, he spotted an interesting rock formation. Pynchon got down from the wagon to get a sample of ancient lava.

Opening page of "The Black Dog" from the *Connecticut Quarterly*, 1898.

His story starts calmly:

> I had been on my knees pounding away for dear life in
> my endeavor to get off a good cabinet specimen and
> had just gotten up to straighten my back, when I noticed
> trotting up the road a dog. I suppose he might've been
> called black, but it was the same degree of blackness
> that you see in an old black hat that has been soaked
> in the rain a good many times . . . [H]e seemed friendly,
> and when I drove on he insisted on following the wagon.
> So I let him go with me for the sake of his good company.

All day long, the dog stayed with Pynchon and his horse
and wagon.

Then we turned back and started for home, the dog running on ahead. I took a great liking to that dog. In the first place he was so quiet. Not once and all that day did I hear him bark, even when a calf beside the road tried to coax him into a fight. And he was so light of foot! Though the roads were very dry, yet I did not see a puff of dust rise from his feet as he trotted along ahead of the horse.

Pynchon turned around for home as the setting sun lit the top of West Peak.

The dog still trotted on ahead until we came to the place where I had met him in the morning. Then he stopped, looked back at me a moment, and quietly vanished into the woods. I stopped and whistled and whistled again, but no dog appeared . . . And this is how I met the Black Dog the first time—for joy.

Fast-forward three years. Pynchon returned to the Hanging Hills in a cold and snowy February 1891. With him was another geologist, Herbert Marshall.

Pynchon and Marshall visited in front of a fireplace at the Winthrop Hotel in nearby Meriden. Marshall was a veteran climber and thoroughly familiar with West Peak.

They chatted about stories of a ghostly black dog that hung out in the Hanging Hills. Recalled Pynchon:

> We talked till late that night, and, as the fire died down to a mass of glowing embers, he told me how he himself had twice seen a black dog upon the mountain, but he laughed at the legends, saying that he did not believe in omens unless they were lucky ones.

The next morning, bright and cold, the pair set out to climb West Peak. The woods were "choked with snow," so they decided to climb the steeper south face of the peak, where trees didn't grow.

It was hard work. It took an hour for them to reach the cliffs themselves. Pynchon noted, "The mass of broken fragments of rock which runs up to the foot of the cliffs affords a fairly good foothold.

"The sharp, bracing air put life into us and we went at the ascent with enthusiasm . . . [I]n the course of an hour we were . . . under the foot of the cliffs." There they found a narrow cleft in the rock, ". . . and then the fun began," Pynchon wrote.

> [B]y scrambling, crawling and wriggling, we got to the top and pulled the camera up after us with a rope, much

to the detriment of the former. Our lunch we left at the foot of the ravine until we should come down.

The lunch, however, would stay untouched.

Pynchon and Marshall had worked up a sweat climbing West Peak and removed their gloves to snap pictures. It was warm in the sun, but as they made their descent into the shadowed ravine, things changed.

So long as we were in the sunlight we went on with some courage, but when we passed into the shadow of those black cliffs, courage seemed to die in our hearts and we struggled on blindly through the drifted snow, hoping . . . almost against hope. Marshall was in the lead, and I was following as best I could, when he suddenly stopped and without a word pointed to the top of the cliff. There, high on the rocks above us, stood a black dog like the one I had seen three years before, except that he looked jet black against the snow wreath above him. As we looked he raised his head and we saw his breath rise steaming from his jaws, but no sound came through the biting air. Once, and only once, he gazed down on us with gleaming eyes and then he bounded back out of sight.

Marshall, white-faced, stood against a rock and said, "I did not believe it before. I believe it now; and it is the third time."

> And then, even as he spoke, the fragment of rock on
> which he stood slipped. There was a cry, a rattle of other
> fragments falling—and I [Pynchon] stood alone.

Stunned, Pynchon stumbled to a farmhouse and sounded the alarm. A party of farmers "brought back the body of poor Marshall." They reported that when they came upon the body, beside it was a black dog, which fled into the shadows of the ravine.

Pynchon's terrifying tale appeared complete with the photos he and Herbert Marshall took that fateful day. An endnote added to its horror, stating that Pynchon fell to his own death in the same spot a few years later. Had he seen the dog a third time? There was no one to tell. More than 130 years since, the story has mushroomed. Even now, media retell the tale of Pynchon's pup.

THE DEMON CAT OF DC

A demon cat haunts the halls of Congress. Yes, you read that correctly. On catlike feet, a ghost wanders the halls of the United States Capitol.

It's said that "DC"—a black cat, of course—has haunted the Capitol since the American Civil War. Newspaper articles from the late 1800s paid witness to the Capitol kitty. Its paw prints are etched in concrete along a walkway outside the Old Supreme Court Chamber, where the highest court in the land met until it got its own building in 1935.

Not only that, said Steve Livengood, director of public programs and chief guide of the United States Capitol Historical Society, but there's another piece of "physical evidence." Livengood pointed to the letters "DC" scratched into Capitol concrete in the Senate terrace west connecting corridor. Were these the work of the Demon Cat?

Livengood is filled with stories about the comings and goings of famous and not-so-famous folks at the Capitol. As he explained, cats roamed the Capitol building to hunt and kill mice. Mice did huge amounts of damage, not to mention the bacteria that lurk in mouse poop. "If you read about old buildings in the eighteenth and nineteenth centuries," Livengood explained, "cats were commonly kept there as 'mousers.'"

Livengood recalled seeing files filled with old newspaper clippings about DC and his haunts. Until, alas, someone decided to

People who walk the halls of Congress can spot paw prints that the Demon Cat left in wet concrete.

toss them. To our good fortune, many 1800s newspapers now appear as digital scans. We have one published in 1898 in Butte (pronounced BYOOT), Montana.

GHOSTS OF THE CAPITOL

THE CAPITOL IN WASHINGTON is probably the most thoroughly haunted building in the world.

No fewer than fifteen well-authenticated ghosts infest it, and some of them are of a more than ordinarily alarming character.

What particularly inspires this last remark is the fact that the Demon Cat is said to have made its appearance again, after many years of absence. This is a truly horrific apparition . . . inasmuch as it has the appearance of an ordinary kitty when first seen, then presently swells up to the size of an elephant before the eyes of the terrified observer.

The Demon Cat, in whose regard testimony of the utmost seeming authenticity was put on record thirty-five years ago, has been missing since 1862. One of the watchmen on duty in the building shot at it then, and it disappeared. Since then, until now, nothing more has been heard of it, though one or two of the older policemen of the Capitol force still speak of the spectral animal in awed whispers.

The Capitol features winding halls and cool cubbyholes, perfect hidey-holes for cats. Visitors snap photos of DC's aging footprints and initials, but Livengood said he'd never met anyone who'd seen the kinesthetic kitty.

Another DC story clawed its way into the *Congressional Record*, a wordy document that's "the official record of the proceedings and debates of the United States Congress," in 1981. The *Record* printed a history of the Capitol Police, including news about DC:

> One of the oldest stories is recounted by newsman John Alexander in his book of Washington ghost tales. It concerns the infamous denizen of the Capitol's lower reaches, "Demon Cat." As the story goes, Demon Cat always waits until its victim is alone. The animal's prey are generally members of the Capitol Police force. One victim told of encountering the infamous cat on a winter's eve. As it walked toward the policeman, the cat began to swell.
>
> The guard felt paralyzed as he stared into the glowing, piercing eyes that came closer and closer and grew larger and larger. The animal swelled to the size of a giant tiger, yet never lost its unmistakable cat-like form. Its purring changed to a ferocious snarl. There was a deafening roar as the monstrous animal leaped—with claws extended—toward its victim. The guard couldn't move. His feet seemed nailed to the floor. He covered

his face with his arms as the giant animal seemed just inches away from landing on him. He screamed.

Nothing happened. The Demon Cat vanished into thin air as the man screamed. The trembling guard stood alone, the corridor deserted, the silence pierced only by his breathing. His limp body was covered in a cold, clammy sweat. He felt drained. The narrow marble hallway now reminded him of a tomb. The guard shuddered, tried to pull himself together, and headed back to his desk. For some reason he just didn't feel like finishing his rounds. This grisly feline was blamed for an elderly guard's fatal heart attack, and the cat is reputed to appear only on the eve of a national tragedy, or upon the changing of presidential administrations!

DC was said to have appeared before the assassinations of Presidents Abraham Lincoln and John F. Kennedy.

Livengood has never laid eyes on DC, but he saw another Capitol ghost many times. You'll read more about that later in this book . . .

THE FISHING CAT OF PARIS

Tourists to the artsy Left Bank neighborhood of Paris, France, enjoy day-tripping along the city's narrowest street, rue du Chat-qui-Pêche (ROO du SHAT-key-PESH). Translated, this means "Street of the Cat Who Fishes," or,

RUE DU CHAT QUI-PÊCHE

5° Arr!

Street art of the Fishing Cat of Paris decorates a wall of the rue du Chat-qui-Pêche.

as we might say in English, "Fishing Cat Street." It's Paris's skinniest street, so skinny that most adults could stretch out their arms and touch buildings on both sides as they walk its twenty-nine-meter length, about ninety-five feet.

But that's not the only tourist attraction on the narrow lane. Le Chat-qui-Pêche, the Fishing Cat, is a ghost! The kitty's tale goes something like this:

> In the 1500s there lived in Paris a canon, a churchman, who practiced alchemy, seeking the secret formula to transform lead into silver or gold. With him lived a sleek black cat with huge paws. This cat was a remarkable fisherman; it had only to dip a big paw into the Seine (SEN) River and, voilà, was immediately rewarded with a fish dinner.
>
> In those days, alchemy was thought of as witchcraft, and the alchemist and his pet were viewed as a kind of witch and his "familiar," a witchy kitty. So three Frenchmen decided to take matters into their own hands and rid the world of at least one troublemaker. They killed the black cat, and at once the alchemist disappeared . . . though after a while the alchemist returned. As for the cat, it returned as well—but in ghostly form—and to this very day fishes the Seine with its huge paws.

If you ever go to Paris, you may look for rue du Chat-qui-Pêche yourself by taking the Métro, Paris's subway. Get off at station Saint-Michel.

THE HISTORIC, GHOSTLY SIMON PURRKINS

In 1998 a stray cat took up residence at the Summit County Historical Society in Akron, Ohio. He hung out there in the society's old stone building known as the Perkins Stone Mansion. The kitty took a name, Simon Purrkins, and befriended the society's director, Paula Moran.

Simon Purrkins hung out by day at the office and at night with his human family. The *Akron Beacon Journal* reported that when Moran moved to Virginia, she took Simon along. He died in late 2012 at the age of fourteen and a half.

Simon Purrkins posed with his original owner, Paula Moran, in 2002.

Simon showed up back in Ohio—as a ghost. Melinda Sedelmeyer, who worked there with volunteers in the old stone house, saw the feline specter.

She was at work one day and wasn't thinking about seeing a cat at all.

> I was cleaning up during the day and walked upstairs to turn out the lights. I remember I took care not to step on the cat. I skirted the cat and four steps later stopped and said, "What the–?" He wasn't a sinister cat like you think of in a movie . . . not really a black, black cat but dark gray, very dark.

Another evening, Sedelmeyer again saw Simon Purrkins as she was leaving the house with her boss. "We're walking down the steps outside, and I jumped out of the way to bypass the cat. I said to Leianne [her boss], 'I didn't want to hurt the cat.'"

The boss hadn't seen anything.

To this day, there are regular Simon Purrkins sightings. Ask Denise Lundell, an accountant who works next door. She saw Simon hanging out in the doorway. But she didn't mention it at home. "My husband," she said, "would have thought I'm crazy."

CHAPTER TWO

GHOSTS GO TO SCHOOL

GHOSTS AT SCHOOL? WHY NOT? LOOK BACK IN THE record book, and you'll find lots of stories of haunted school-houses. Today, haints and haunts are *still* said to ghost from class to class. Ghosts go to school all over the world . . .

A CORKER OF A GHOST

It was just as the calendar flipped from September to October in 2017 when a high school principal in Cork, Ireland, went into work. It was a Monday, but Deerpark CBS (Christian Brothers School) wasn't in session. The principal, Kevin Barry, strolled into the building, only to find a locker door wide open and stuff strewn all over the floor.

On October 2, the school posted on its Facebook page, "Anyone have the number for ghostbusters?" and a YouTube

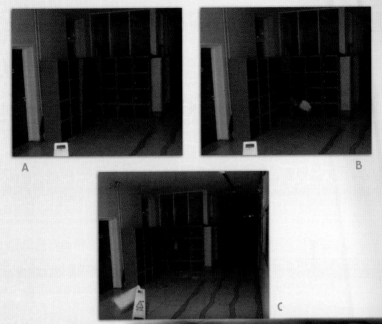

A

B

C

Here are three images captured by the Deerpark school surveillance cameras, posted on the school's Facebook page. It shows swinging doors, shifting lockers (A), a falling notebook (B), and a sliding sign (C), all moving without any humans present.

video of knocked-down signs and flying notebooks went viral. Was this a prank or a poltergeist at play?

Ever since, deputy principal Aaron Wolfe said, "We've been very busy."

Deerpark, at the time a boys-only Catholic high school, was "crazy with the ghost." There had been a céilí (KAY-lee), an Irish dance party, at the school the Saturday night before Barry found the mess. Did pranksters get into the school hallways and disrupt things? Or did someone purposely fake the ghostly visit?

On October 31, Deerpark posted a second, equally creepy video of more freakish events: sliding chairs, a flying book-bag, and a poster falling off a wall.

The chase was on. A film crew flew in from Japan and rigged up electronics to sense whether a ghost had enrolled at Deerpark. "At four a.m.," Wolfe said, "they heard all kinds of noises going off." The crew brought a Japanese comedian along to provide color commentary, but that didn't work out. The man was spooked by all the sounds, including random piano banging, and he refused to keep working. Even weirder, when the Japanese got home, they discovered that their tapes had been erased. They used Deerpark's own tapes for their program.

Deerpark also recruited an American ghost hunter who declared she'd never come across a building as haunted as this.

"Doors opened on their own—doors with latches that you push down as you open them—and that's hard to do," Wolfe added. "I swear to God, this happened several times."

Just as creepy was the "toilet door that locked itself from the inside." In Ireland and other lands, "toilets" are often small rooms closed in from floor to ceiling, so there's no getting in except through a doorway. "Our boys don't use it anymore," Wolfe said.

The deputy principal had been at the Deerpark school only a few years. But he learned it had a long, eerie history.

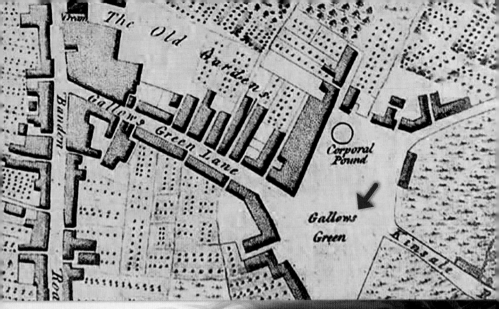

An old map of Cork shows Gallows Green more than two hundred and fifty years ago.

At some point Deerpark had hosted a show of exotic birds in the school hall, and one of the birds' caretakers spent the night there to keep an eye on things.

Noted Wolfe: "At five a.m. the man clearly heard the sound of a trumpet playing the military 'last call.'" (In the United States, we call that "taps," which officially ends the day on army posts and is played at military funerals.) Sometimes passersby at the school see weird lights and hear freakish alarms.

"I swear, it was insane," Wolfe said. Then Wolfe, who also teaches English and literature, got another history lesson. The land where the Deerpark school now sits once had a more sinister purpose. The area was known as Gallows Green, the site of public executions for years.

So…it made sense that Deerpark became "Fearpark," at least once a year. That would be around Halloween, when Deerpark hosted a fundraising party for the school. That tradition continues, though Deerpark CBS made a big change in 2019, when it welcomed girls as students. It has a new name: Coláiste Éamann Rís (ko-LESH-tuh AY-mon REESH), Irish for Edmund Rice College (School).

BATHROOM HAUNTS

Deerpark isn't the only school with a creeped-out restroom. You might have heard about Moaning Myrtle, the bathroom ghost Harry Potter encounters early on at Hogwarts School of Witchcraft and Wizardry. But Myrtle is in a

Ghosts haunt school restrooms all across Japan!

book. In Japan, kids (and adults) will swear they've met a real ghost, the "third floor, third stall" specter of a little girl who haunts a toilet.

To meet Hanako-san, as she's known formally, simply visit the girl's bathroom on the third floor in any number of schools. Knock three times on the door of the third stall. (In Japan, many bathroom stalls are like small rooms and have walls that run floor to ceiling.) When the door opens, there will be Hanako, often wearing a red skirt.

You can't be sure which version of Hanako will greet you. This depends on where you live. Sometimes she's looking for a playmate. In other places, maybe not. Or, she's transformed into a three-headed lizard. Often her bloody hand might try to seize you. They say if Hanako grasps you in fury, she will drag you to hell through the toilet.

RAGE AT THE YORK INDUSTRIAL RAGGED SCHOOL

Homeless, orphaned kids often lived on the street in towns and cities in Great Britain during the 1800s. Danger lurked everywhere. Churchgoing men and women stepped up to help out, with dreams and plans to educate these "waifs" so they could hold respectable jobs.

By the mid-1800s, industrial schools—boarding schools for vagrant children—sprang up in slums, where the poorest people lived and lawlessness ruled. One such school opened in York, northern England's industrial center. Aptly named the York Industrial Ragged School, the school sat in the city's once-grand Bedern section. But when the school opened in 1848, Bedern had become a slum.

The program taught hands-on skills so that students could find work. Boys learned shoemaking, carpentry, and tailoring. Girls learned needlework and housekeeping.

Depending on whose website you read, it seems that the place first ran under one George Pimm, hired by well-meaning people to run the school. But greedy, evil Pimm had everyone fooled. He beat and starved the children in his care.

Kids at ragged schools ate breakfast, lunch, and dinner crammed along tables like these.

The best research on this gruesome story comes from a British historian named Rupert Matthews, who has chased ghost stories all over the world. Matthews says details on the gory story are up for grabs:

> Quite how bad the man's regime was is a matter of conjecture. The worst that was proved against him was that he had given overly vicious beatings to children and had pilfered city funds to pay for his drinking and gambling.

But a website from the BBC, the government-owned media company in the United Kingdom, claims that when children died in the ragged school, Pimm stashed their bodies there. Pimm, they say, was paid *per capita*. (That's Latin for "per person," literally "by the head.")

> When a child died, the church would give them a Christian burial and cross the name off the school list. Hence, George Pimm would lose an allowance for the dead child. So to ensure he lost no further subsidies, Pimm began to hide the dead children within the grounds and walls of the school.

It sounds as though the authorities never thought to do a head count of *living* children at the school.

In time, the evil Pimm got his comeuppance, when the posthumous sighs and sounds of these waifs drove him to insanity. Pimm's pitiful victims had become ghosts. The former headmaster expired in an asylum, a fearsome place that housed the mentally ill.

The old ragged school building was torn down to make way for new buildings in the later 1800s. These, too, were torn down after more than a hundred years. All over Europe, cities have piled up to the point where archaeologists check out an area before new buildings arise. That's what happened when archaeologists excavated the old site of the York Industrial Ragged School. Writes Matthews:

> Several of those working on the site felt unaccountably uneasy, as if they were being watched. One man had a particularly unnerving experience. He was busy on the dig when he felt somebody tap him urgently and insistently on the shoulder, but when he turned around, there was nobody there. When he undressed that evening his wife told him to look at his back in the mirror. On the shoulder where he had felt the taps were parallel bruises, as if he had been gripped hard by the fingers of a child-sized hand.

Ouch.

"IT'S A HOLIDAY, THANK THE GHOSTS"

Thank the ghosts for school holidays? In northeastern India, students got a few days off from classes thanks to an evil spirit.

On Monday, July 15, 2007, the *Telegraph* newspaper of India reported that Toiba High School in the state of West Bengal had closed for four days. Twelve of its female pupils had had fainting spells.

In this village of Kusumgram, plenty of local residents fretted about a ghost in the old mansion next door to the school. One parent told the paper that "everyone in the village was aware of the presence of an evil spirit in the haunted house. But the spirit never disturbed anyone. 'We don't really know what is happening. We are scared and don't want to send our children to school.'" Caretakers for the old house denied that anything fishy was going on inside.

CHAPTER THREE

WEIRD WRAITHS IN WHITE SPACES

ON JUNE 12, 1945, PRESIDENT HARRY TRUMAN SAT DOWN in the White House to write a letter to his wife, Bess. Truman was brand-new at the nation's biggest job. President Franklin D. Roosevelt had died without warning on April 12.

Truman had written hundreds of letters to his beloved Bess over the years. She and their college-age daughter, Margaret, were at home in Missouri when he wrote to them. In his letter, he reflected on matters of state—and a few other tidbits about past presidents . . .

> Just two months ago today, I was a reasonably happy and contented Vice-President . . . But things have changed so much it hardly seems real.

I sit here in this old house and work on foreign affairs, read reports, and work on speeches—all the while listening to the ghosts walk up and down the hallway and even right here in the study. The floors pop and the drapes move back and forth—I can just imagine old Andy and Teddy having an argument over Franklin. Or James Buchanan and Franklin Pierce deciding which was the more useless to the country. And when Millard Fillmore and Chester Arthur join in for place and show the din is almost unbearable. But I still get some work done.

Harry Truman was known for his straight talk. When Bess was away with Margaret the next year, he shared more White House news.

President Harry S. Truman, his wife Bess (left), and their daughter, Margaret (center), waved from the rear platform of a passenger train as they crossed the United States.

I slept well but hot, and some mosquitoes bit my hands and face. Night before last I went to bed at nine o'clock after shutting all my doors. At four o'clock I was awakened by three distinct knocks on my bedroom door. I jumped up and put on my bathrobe, opened the door, and no one [was] there. Went out and looked up and down the hall, looked into your room and Margie's. Still no one. Went back to bed after locking the doors and there were footsteps in your room, whose door I'd left open. Jumped and looked and no one there! The damned place is haunted, sure as shootin'. Secret Service said not even a watchman was up here at that hour.

You and Margie had better come back and protect me before some of these ghosts carry me off.

The bumps in the night kept on coming. Floors crumbled and draperies swayed. A leg of Margaret's piano popped through a floorboard and through the ceiling below. Truman's good humor turned to anger. But an election was coming, so the president stayed quiet until he won on November 3, 1948, which surprised both Truman and the nation.

The architect of the White House and other experts poked around and decided that the White House was indeed sinking and falling down. Truman's assistant John R. Steelman explained. "People all over the country are asking, 'Why is the White House suddenly so unsafe?'"

Steelman went on to say that the White House, like the city, stood on swampy ground. Previous restorations put too many stresses on the old building, and the men in charge had made big mistakes. So the Trumans moved out. It took three years for the executive mansion to be gutted and rebuilt.

Something weird happened more than fifty years later. In 2008 an observant reader of a Truman biography spotted a peculiar image in an old photo in the book. The photograph was of the White House basement back in 1949. Abbie Rowe, a National Park Service employee, had taken the shot as he made a pictorial record of the White House restoration. A paranormal expert, Joshua P. Warren, declared that the image in the photo was none other than Abraham Lincoln's ghost.

TRUMAN WASN'T THE FIRST . . .

Not as well-known is the ghost of a teenage boy who prowled the White House in 1911. President William Howard Taft was in office. Taft's military aide, Archibald Butt, penned a letter to his sister about the ghoulish lad, whom staff had nicknamed "the Thing."

> It seems that the White House is haunted . . . The ghost,
> it seems, is a young boy—from its description, I should
> think about fourteen or fifteen years old . . . They say
> that the first knowledge one has of the presence of the
> Thing is a slight pressure on the shoulder, as of [sic]

someone were leaning over your shoulder to see what you might be doing.

Taft's aide, however, became the butt of Taft's anger when he heard the story. The president, a very large man, became a mountain of "a towering rage ... he thinks it will be a very serious thing to have the story get out among the people of the country." Taft told Butt to tell the White House house-keeper that the first person to leak a story about the Thing would lose his or her job.

In 1913 the *Washington Herald* ran an article with an alto-gether snarky headline: "White House Is Notorious Haunt of Ghosts; Nobody Ever Minded Living There, However." The paper didn't mention the Thing, but it did provide word of an early haint decked out in colonial garb. The ghost was female, the *Herald* said.

> The most interesting of these specters is that of a woman with a cap of antique pattern, a garment resembling a lace shawl, and widely distended hoop skirt. She is seen not at midnight, as is customary with most well-regulated ghosts, but just before daybreak, gliding slowly along the wide hallway which extends lengthwise through the middle of the White House. It is always from the west end to the east that she moves, and when she reaches the closed double doors, which give entrance to the East

Room, she passes through them, as if they offered no obstacle, and vanishes.

Nobody can tell with positiveness, of course, but the supposition is that the phantom is that of Abigail Adams, the first mistress of the White House.

THE SADDEST GHOST EVER?

It *ghosts* without saying that Abraham Lincoln haunts the White House. Every part of Lincoln's life was touched with sadness. At a young age he lost his mother, followed later by his sweetheart and two of his sons. His wife, Mary Todd Lincoln, was deeply troubled, and Lincoln suffered with her. In April 1865 he was assassinated just as he looked forward to "binding up the nation's wounds" after the Civil War. Lincoln's ghost is said to show up in times of national crisis.

The *Washington Herald* said in 1913 that Lincoln "is always seen walking up the stairs. It is impossible to mistake his tall, awkward figure and shambling gait. When he gets to the top, he looks around, smiles sadly, and disappears." Lincoln's preferred spot made sense. In 1913, the presidential offices were on the second floor, accessed by a double flight of stairs.

Today Lincoln's ghost haunts the Lincoln Bedroom, the most famous bedroom in the White House. The room once served as the president's study; it didn't take its current name until Harry Truman was in office. A giant, heavy bed of dark wood was moved there along with other heavy, carved Victorian furniture that was popular in the mid-1800s. The irony is that the president probably never slept in that bed, but the room made a perfect landing pad for ghosts.

So who are the famous folks who met Lincoln's ghost? Queen Wilhelmina of the Netherlands, for one, who slept in the Lincoln Bedroom during a White House visit during World War II. She heard a knock on the door and opened it, only to meet the ghost. The queen, whose bravery during the war was unquestioned, fainted dead away.

Supposedly Queen Wilhelmina asked for a different room during her next visits.

The Lincoln Bedroom and its ghost have welcomed illustrious White House guests for many years.

In the 2000s Barbara and Jenna Bush, twin daughters of President George W. Bush, were college students when their dad was in office. The Bush girls made frequent visits to the White House. In a double interview later, the twins revealed that—more than once—music played through the old fireplaces in the rooms where they slept. Once it was a woman singing opera, and another time, 1920s jazz. "The hair on the back of our neck was standing up," Jenna Bush recalled.

THE ADAMS APPARITION

Presidential ghosts haunt other spaces, too. One is the apparition of John Quincy Adams, son of John and Abigail Adams. He was the sixth president of the United States and the only president ever who, after his term, returned

A photo of the White House amid remodeling in 1949 reveals Abraham Lincoln's ghost in the basement.

to Congress. An intense and standoffish man, the former president worked to change the way Congress did business in the 1830s and 1840s.

At issue was slavery, the most controversial subject ever to divide America. Adams opposed the enslavement of African people.

John Quincy Adams cherished his role as congressman and the opportunities it offered for him to make real change in American life. When he held the floor during debates, he walked about waving his arms to emphasize his words.

Adams died on the job. He had a stroke as the House was in session and collapsed in the chamber. His colleagues carried him into the nearby Speaker's room and laid him on a sofa, where he died.

Steve Livengood, chief tour of the Capitol Historical Society, surprised me when I interviewed him about DC, the Capitol's Demon Cat. Livengood affirmed that he's never seen the ghostly feline, but he had more to say:

> I do a lot of evening programs and [afterward] I like to walk in the Capitol and walk alone . . . I'm walking back to communicate with spirits who are there . . . I have seen John Quincy Adams. He was known as "Old Man Eloquent." He never acknowledges my presence . . . I don't hear him, but he is clearly giving a speech.

With grand gestures, Adams's ghost is hammering away at a topic. Adams opposed the United States going to war against Mexico in 1846. "He objected to giving medals to [army] generals following the Mexican War," Livengood explained. Adams was giving others a piece of his mind on the subject when he died.

Apparently, his ghost has kept at it.

President John Quincy Adams's ghost still lectures in the room where he died.

THE WHITE TOWER'S HEADLESS QUEEN

About one hundred years ago, readers of the Sunday *New York Times*, a newspaper that takes itself very seriously, saw a brief article about a ghost. Buried in the middle of its densely printed page seven was this:

GHOST OF ANNE BOLEYN AT THE TOWER

LONDON, Sept 18.—In spite of official frowns and attempts to suppress the chatter, it has leaked out that the detachment of Foot Guards quartered at the Tower of London swear the sentries on night duty have seen the ghost of Anne Boleyn, the second unfortunate wife of the much-married King Henry VIII, whom he caused to be beheaded on May 19, 1536. The ghost of Queen Anne Boleyn is only supposed to appear on the eve of the death of a member of the Royal family, and, therefore, the matter has been made the occasion for considerable gossip.

Anne Boleyn (pronounced BO-lin). Second wife of England's King Henry VIII. Perhaps you've heard of him. Monarch from 1509 to 1547, Henry Tudor was the king who married six times.

When Henry had been king for some sixteen or seventeen years, he got restless. His wife, Catherine of Aragon, had borne Henry a perfectly fine daughter, Princess Mary. But Henry wanted a Tudor son to rule after him.

Then along came Anne Boleyn. Sometime in the late 1520s, Anne, of good family and well educated (for a girl), caught Henry's eye. He set his statesmen and churchmen in motion to allow him to divorce Catherine so that he could marry Anne. As for Anne, she wouldn't settle, as they say, for being simply another of Henry's girlfriends. She kept the upper hand in the courtship, and Henry married her in 1533.

Imagine Henry's—and Anne's—disappointment when their firstborn child was a girl, Elizabeth. She was sent to the countryside to be raised. Anne became pregnant twice more with Henry's children, but one she miscarried, and the next, a boy, was stillborn. Henry, impatient as ever to get a son, cast his eyes on Jane Seymour, one of Queen Anne's ladies-in-waiting.

But first, he had to dump Anne. Henry's henchmen worked up all kinds of lies about her, especially that she had plotted his downfall. Poor Anne was tried in a court like any kind of criminal.

Anne didn't deserve the verdict she received: Death. By beheading, as was fit for a queen.

Anne was imprisoned in the Tower of London. She and her ladies lived in the shadow of the White Tower, the stone

Anne Boleyn met her death with grace and dignity, but she returned to haunt the Tower of London.

inner keep deep in the castle grounds. North of the White Tower was a scaffold. It was meant for her.

On May 19, 1536, Anne and her ladies walked to her scaffold. A French executioner, chosen for his skill with a sword, stood at the ready. Her dark hair wrapped up, the queen knelt and the swordsman did his duty. As was the custom, he held up Anne's head for the gathered crowd to see.

Anne's ladies found an old arrow box and laid Anne's body therein, her head tucked to one side. Nearby stood the Chapel Royal of St. Peter ad Vincula. The arrow box was shoved under the altar floor.

Eleven days later, Henry married Jane Seymour. Bells rang all over England when she gave birth to a son who became King Edward VI. He didn't live very long, and it was Henry's daughters, Mary and Elizabeth, who ruled thereafter.

It's no wonder that, head under her arm, Anne Boleyn haunts the Tower of London. A chilling account appeared in 1882, when the author, a Mr. "Spectre-Stricken" shared his tale about a military officer on night duty at the Tower.

> Well, an old friend of mine, Captain _____, of the regiment _____, was one evening going the rounds with the sentry when he saw a light burning in the chapel. He pointed it out to the other, and asked what it meant.
>
> "I don't know what it means, sir, but I have often

seen that and stranger things here of nights," was the sentinel's reply.

Again and again my friend looked at the window, and each time the light gleamed through the darkness. Determined to ascertain the cause, Captain _____ procured a ladder, placed it against the chapel wall, mounted it, and gazed in on a scene that thrilled his every nerve. Slowly down the aisle moved a stately procession of knights and ladies, attired in ancient costumes; and in front walked an elegant female, whose face was averted from him, but whose figure greatly resembled the one he had seen in reputed portraits of Anne Boleyn. After having repeatedly paced the chapel, the entire procession, together with the light, disappeared. So deeply was my friend impressed with the seeming reality of the scene, that not till then did he discover he had been gazing in on a phantom crowd.

So Anne's face was "averted." Did her ghost have a face or head at all?

And, yes, one month after the *New York Times* ran that short article, a member of Great Britain's vast royal family did die. She was Princess Mary Adelaide of Cambridge, first cousin to Queen Victoria and Queen Elizabeth II's great-grandmother.

CHAPTER FOUR

GHOSTLY HITCHHIKERS, BANDITS, AND A LADY IN WHITE

AS YOU TRAVEL HIGHWAYS AND BYWAYS, YOU MIGHT JUST meet a ghost looking for a lift. Sometimes it's a nice one, and sometimes not.

THE VANISHING HITCHHIKER

One of the most roadworthy ghosts is the vanishing hitch-hiker. There are lots of reports of unwary drivers picking up someone on the road, only to find that their guest rider was a phantom. This has been going on since *way* back to horse-and-buggy days.

Here's one sighting, written down by a story collector named Delana Good in 1967. It was told to her by Jane Albright, who was probably a teenager when she spoke of a vanishing hitchhiker. This is how the story was typed up and placed in a file of papers more than fifty years ago:

These two boys were driving down a country road in southern Indiana when they saw a young girl walking along the road. It was raining pretty hard and beginning to get kind of cold. The boys pulled over and asked the girl if she wanted a ride. She told them where she wanted to go and then got in the back of the car. She began to shiver, and one of the boys took off his jacket and put it over her shoulders. They drove the girl to her home and helped her to the front door. The boys rang the doorbell and the girl's father answered the door. When he asked what they wanted, the boys were shocked to find out that the girl was gone. The boys were really upset, so the man asked them in. He was sure they were mistaken, though, because he explained to them that his daughter had been dead for two years. However, the boys described her perfectly and began to get more anxious. The man wanted to prove them wrong, so he drove them to the graveyard where his daughter was buried. When they came to the girl's grave, the boy's jacket was hanging across the tombstone.

Sightings of vanishing hitchhikers have roots that grow deep. There's an old Swedish story from 1602 about a pair of travelers who met a "'nice and lovely' girl on the road who did various magical things." Before she vanished, she left them with "a prophecy of wars and plagues." Scary stuff!

In the county of Shropshire, England, a ghost named Madam Piggott liked to jump onto a passing horse and tag along until the rider managed to push her off or cross over some kind of stream or river that would do the job for him. As an old magazine explained, "The merest tyro [newbie] in legendary lore can tell you that a spirit may never by any possibility whatsoever cross a running stream. Ghosts never 'cross the bourne [boundary].'"

In America, ghosts have accompanied unwary party-goers to country barn dances and city discos. Others, like the Indiana girl, have thumbed rides during heavy storms. Beware the stranger you don't know!

Sometimes, though, vanishing hitchhikers show up to help people out. Travelers might meet a stranger who begs them to go find a doctor or a priest to care for someone who's dying.

Other times, the ghost turns up to warn of danger down the road. In England there's a story about a railway ghost that appeared to an engine driver (engineer) on a locomotive. It starts like this: "I was driving the 8:30 train to the North, and left King's Cross four minutes behind time. I can't tell you what it was, but I never felt nervousness but once on an engine, and that was on the night I'm talking about."

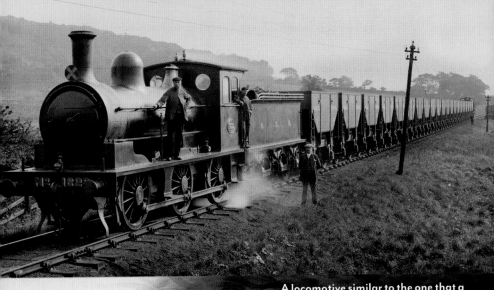

A locomotive similar to the one that a ghost took over to save a passenger train from a deadly accident.

The engine driver claimed he was ready to swear before any judge what he saw.

It was just when we were passing through Hatfield when . . . a man stepped from platform to the footplate, just as easily as though we were not travelling about fifty-five miles an hour . . . It was the saddest face I ever come across. The eyes seemed to look you through and through; and when on top of that I saw that he was all in black, I never was so afraid in my life.

His fireman, the man who stoked the steam engine with coal, noticed nothing.

I soon noticed that the strange-comer never went to any
other part of the footplate except to the spot whereon
I stood, and he even hedged up so close to me that I
went cold all over, and my feet were like lumps of ice. I
think I must have acted mechanically, for I watched the
man put his hand upon the regulator, and I put mine
with his. The touch of it was like the touch of snow, but
I couldn't loose it, and before I knew what I'd done, the
steam was cut off and the train was slowing.

Both the engine driver and fireman saw in front of them
that "the home signal stood for line clear."

Something had made the engine driver "stop that express,
and stop her I did outside Hitchin Station."

. . . Heaven alone knows how, but it proved to be for a
great deal. There were two trucks across the main line,
and although the signals were off, the way was blocked,
so that me and the passengers behind me wouldn't be
living to tell the story if I hadn't been compelled to pull
up as I did . . .

If there's no engine power, then the vanishing-hitchhiker
tale goes walking on the beach, like this sighting in Somalia.
The transcriber, college professor John William Johnson,

was visiting Somali National University to lecture on legends about vanishing hitchhikers. To the Indiana professor's surprise, a Somali student insisted that such stories couldn't be mere legends, because he'd heard one right there in Somalia.

Young Ali went to study for his BA in the United States. He had a girlfriend back home in the Somali Democratic Republic, and he wrote to her regularly and she to him. He was in the States for four years and finally finished his course of studies and took his degree; so, he returned home to Somalia on an airplane, landing in the coastal capital of Mogadishu.

His girlfriend, Fadumo, met him at the airport, and they were obviously very happy to see each other after so long a time. They spent the whole day together, and in the evening, they went to the al-Uruba Hotel to dance at a nightclub in the basement. When it got very late, Ali walked Fadumo home along the beach, where it was a bit cold, so he lent her his jacket, which she draped across her shoulders. He then started home himself, realizing after parting with Fadumo that he had forgotten to retrieve his jacket. "No matter," he thought. "I will get it in the morning." The next morning he went to Fadumo's house and knocked on the door.

Her father invited him in and summoned the whole

family to come and greet him. After a while, Ali asked Fadumo's father where she was, thinking that she had slept in because of their late-night escapade.

"Oh, Ali," said her father, "I have very bad news. Fadumo was killed in a car crash two years ago. I am sorry to greet you with these sad tidings."

"Impossible!" shouted Ali. "I spent the whole day with her yesterday. We even went to the al-Uruba nightclub last evening! I . . . I . . . I have her letters for the past four years!"

Nothing would console Ali, so Fadumo's father decided to take him to the Dhigfer Cemetery to her grave to prove to him that she had passed on. Ali agreed and sat quietly in the car as they drove up the hill to the cemetery. When they arrived at Fadumo's grave, Ali and Fadumo's father were astounded to find Ali's coat lying atop her grave.

Somalia and Indiana are 8,170 miles (13,145 meters) apart. Funny (or not) how folks from different walks of life tell the same kinds of ghost stories . . .

THE BOY UNDER THE BRIDGE

There's a haunted highway near Milford, New Jersey, that has driven people nuts for years. It's Clinton Road, a winding way that tracks through the woods and promises all kinds of creepiness—ruins of a demolished castle, abandoned ironworks, and a Dead Man's Curve.

Clinton Road's most famous haint lives under a normal-looking stone bridge now flanked by steel guardrails. The ghost, a boy, lurks about the fast-running stream below. Legend says that if you pull over and toss a coin into the white rushing water, the ghost will hurl it back. Hmm ... there's a ghost that refuses to make your wishes come true! Just ask someone named Dina, from nearby Milford, New Jersey, who left a message on the website Weird N.J.:

My friends and I decided to find out for ourselves what is true and what is not. We went to the bridge and threw

Dead Man's Curve along Clinton Road bridges a creek that's home to a ghostly boy.

The Boy under the Bridge appears to those who toss coins into his watery home.

a quarter off. Not but a minute later you hear the *bloop,* as if you dropped the quarter in again. The water filled with ripples, and a child's reflection appeared. I flew back to the car. That scared all of us.

LA LLORONA, THE WOMAN WHO WEEPS

For generations, parents in parts of Latin America and the U.S. Southwest have sent kids out to play with a warning:

"Stay away from that stream! Don't wander by the river! Get out of that arroyo (creek bed)! La Llorona might get you!"

La Llorona, the Woman Who Weeps. A ghostly woman haunting rivers, streams, and lakes. Sometimes she wears a black dress and sports sharp fingernails. In other places, she dresses in a flowing white gown, hair streaming down her back. Her shrill screams sound like a wildcat's growl. Her face is stained with tears. She wanders and weeps and tears at her hair.

La Llorona (LAH yoh-ROH-nah) weeps because she lost her children. She's on the move, all the while calling, "Ay! Mis hijos! Ay! Mis hijos!" (Iee Mees E-hos, "Oh, my children!")

Her children should be right by her side. But they are not.

La Llorona killed them. Why depends on what story you hear and where you live, as well. One version says that the Weeping Woman lived happily with her husband and two sons until her husband left her for a younger, prettier woman. Out of her mind with anger, La Llorona drowned her children in a river. Or abandoned them beside a flooding creek. Or stabbed them with a dagger. When the woman herself dies, she's turned away at heaven's door because she cannot explain where her children are.

A woodblock print captures La Llorona's grief as she wades through water seeking her children, who are forever lost to her.

There are as many versions of this horrible story as you have fingers and toes. Among many

A carving of Coatlicue, or Serpent Skirt, which is a manifestation of the goddess Cihuacoatl, the Snake Woman, inspired fear among her Aztec followers.

Latinx families, La Llorona is the quintessential ghost. A classic!

Some ethnographers, scholars who study human cultures, trace La Llorona back to the Aztecs. These native people lived across Mexico when Spaniards made contact in the late 1400s and early 1500s. The Aztecs called their ancient goddess Cihuacoatl, the Snake Woman.

But why did Cihuacoatl (see-HWA-ko-AHTL) hold so much power? This fearsome goddess was one angry woman, because she foretold the future. And for her people, the future wasn't bright. The Spaniards would impose their way of life upon the Aztecs, as they did across their global empire.

But that was only a beginning. As old ways died away and new ways evolved, so did La Llorona's story. Past memories of snake goddesses blended with Spanish legends of mistreated women who went on to murder their loved ones. One account says that the Spanish general Hernán Cortés didn't speak Náhuatl, so a beautiful, upper-class Aztec woman became his translator. Her name was *La Malinche* (Lah ma-LEEN-che).

Cortés, ignoring thoughts of his wife, fell in love with a woman now known as La Malinche. She became his concubine, and they had a son. When he was to return to his wife, who lived far off, he planned to take their son with him. Enraged, the translator killed her boy. Left with no one to love, she died—and became La Malinche.

La Malinche became the symbol of a traitor; she had "sold out" by getting mixed up with Cortés, the invader.

Sometime, somehow, the story of La Malinche became entangled with that of La Llorona. Look at Hispanic books, films, and pop music, and there's La Malinche right along with La Llorona.

The fearsome Weeping Woman certainly wept in Emporia, Kansas.

A Hispanic American poet named Antonia Quintana Pigno grew up with girlhood memories of La Llorona. She transcribed Hispanic stories told in Emporia and found that the ghost had traveled with families to Kansas. Just as the Weeping Woman haunted big cities like Los Angeles and Tucson, so did she haunt the very creek that ran behind a church in Emporia!

Said one person who was interviewed:

> She supposedly drowned her daughter or son. At night she would go by the creek and would cry. And she would jump some little kid, try to steal some kid, so she could get back her son or daughter. And I was afraid of her, and I didn't know who she was. And some of us would play out where we used to go to school, at St. Catherine's. And there would be a creek back there, and we would go down, and one time I thought I saw the Llorona, but you know, I was just afraid.

Another interviewee stated that La Llorona was a ploy used by the Spanish to keep Mexican people afraid to leave their homes at night. In other words, La Llorona was a false idea, "nada . . . mas' una imaginacion"—nothing more than imagination.

But another insisted that La Llorona hung out by a golf course, too:

> Well, where we used to live . . . And of course the golf course went down to the river. The edge of it was at the river. And we used to, we were such scaredy-cats anyway, we used to actually hear her cry. And you know that wasn't true, but a lot of times you hear the wind, and

my uncle was the good one for telling about the Llorona. She died, and she was still crying looking for her baby. And that's why she still cries at night . . . Cause you can see the trees now, and the little creek that goes by. And every once in a while I think about it.

Today, La Llorona holds strong for Antonia Quintana Pigno. "La Llorona is a fixture in the Mexican and Mexican American communities . . . I was very surprised and delighted when I learned the participants told their stories of La Llorona set in their own particular neighborhoods."

Added Pigno: "I can't stress how important she is to our culture; perhaps as important as Santa [Claus] is here in this country."

NED KELLY: BUSHRANGER

On the vast continent of Australia, one man stands alone in history as both a criminal and hero. His name was Ned Kelly.

Kelly was born into a poor Irish Australian family in 1854. His father, convicted of stealing two pigs back in Ireland, had been forced to emmigrate to Australia, where he settled in the state of Victoria.

Young Ned Kelly grew up when Great Britain still ruled Ireland. There was no love lost between the Irish and British,

Ned Kelly stood in chains shortly before he was executed.

even on the other side of the world. His father and other family members got in trouble with the authorities in Australia, as well.

Kelly's father died when he was eleven, and the young boy became the "man" of the house. He had an "attitude" and was what middle-class Australians call a "larrikin," a low-class rebel or hooligan. Ned ran afoul of the law when his sister caught the eye of a policeman. Ned's sister didn't fancy the lawman, and when the cop kept pursuing her, that's when trouble started.

Ned, his brother Dan, and two friends took to robbing banks and hiding out in the forest—bushranging, as Australians say. Sometime during his brief career, Kelly and his gang shot three police officers dead. Now Ned Kelly had a big price on his head, and deservedly so.

And yet Kelly became a sort of hero, Robin Hood–style, to his fellow Aussies.

"Really confusing," said Craig Powell, a paranormal investigator based in Sydney, Australia's biggest city. "Was he a criminal, or was he out to protect his family?"

Ned Kelly's robberies rose to mythical heights when he and his gang fashioned themselves suits of armor. As Kelly bashed his way through the bush, the clanking noise he made raised the hackles on his victims. Some who saw him thought the armored man was a robber ghost.

Ned's sorry saga came to an end in 1880 when a sheriff's posse lay in wait for him outside a small hotel in Glenrowan,

Ned Kelly's armor fooled some into thinking he was a ghost. This image of his fight and capture appeared in the *Australian Illustrated News* on July 17, 1880.

Victoria. Three of the Kelly gang died. Ned was shot in the legs, rehabbed so that he could stand trial, and sentenced to death. He was hanged, "legs kicking the wind," in the Old Melbourne Gaol (jail) on November 11, 1880. His last words: "Such is life."

REACHING OUT TO A BUSHRANGER

Craig Powell, a past professional rugby player in Australia, is a tour guide climbing the Sydney Harbour Bridge by day and paranormal investigator by night. In 2016 Powell and others went in search of Ned Kelly's ghost. Powell, by now a veteran ghost hunter, had immersed himself in Kelly's story.

> We put ourselves in situations. Sooner or later you start clicking on to things. It's a matter of timing and putting yourself in the environment. It's like training yourself mentally—practice, practice . . . I can get the vibes pretty quick.

The team traveled to several locations associated with the bushranger. One evening, at the very site in Glenrowan where Ned Kelly was taken down, Powell experienced an unusually strong sense that he was in touch with a ghost. "Vibing," he calls it. He had brought along a replica of Kelly's helmet and held it in front of him.

When a ghostly voice whispered, Powell thought it might be Kelly's. "It was as if Ned Kelly was sitting there with his armor in front of me." For Powell, the encounter was "really emotional."

Powell's research of Ned Kelly and the others in his posse had paid off. "When we immerse ourselves in the history of a place, our rewards are so much better!" he says. On that particu-

Paranormal investigator Craig Powell

lar night, Powell received a painful payout for his research. After multiple pleas—"Is that you, Ned? . . . Is there anything you want to tell us Ned?"—the ghost replied. It left a four-inch scratch down the middle of Powell's back.

Craig Powell was no stranger to the paranormal. He first saw a ghost when he was sixteen. Powell was babysitting, caring for his brand-new baby nephew at his sister's house, when the ghost of a woman appeared in the house. And no one believed him.

This was in the early 1990s, before ghost shows became popular on TV and before the Internet was up and running. So off to the library Craig Powell flew.

Books and encyclopedias there schooled Powell in the weird, wild world of ghosts. "I'm reading and researching and learning," he recalls. He still does.

As for his disbelieving family back when Powell was a teenage babysitter? His sister and her family moved out of that house nine months after Powell's creepy encounter.

GHOSTS—A MUSICAL SELECTION

Haunted museums, libraries, parks, concert halls—you name it, and you'll find a ghost or two attached to the building or what stood there before. A case in point: Cincinnati, Ohio, where ghosts haunt the city's Music Hall. When it opened in 1875, Cincinnatians boasted about the largest stage between New York City and Chicago.

Fans of a different sort crowd into Music Hall, too. Ghost fans. You might think of a 125 year-old building as *old*, but there's lots more history *under* Music Hall.

In its early days, Cincinnatians lived (and died) through several epidemics of cholera. This waterborne disease made people sick with fever and rampant diarrhea. Hundreds died, and many children were left without parents.

The city built an orphan asylum, a big group home, to house these parentless kids. The building stood on Elm Street, where Music Hall stands today. Next door was a graveyard called a potter's field, a burial place for poor people and unclaimed bodies.

When digging began for Music Hall in 1876, boxes of bones were packed up and moved. During restorations in 1927 and 1988, more bones appeared.

Spirits of orphaned kids and other cholera victims haunted their old digs. Scott Santangelo, who directed operations at Music Hall, tells that a ghostly little girl has warned guests away from the basement. In 2012 she showed up during a performance of an *American Idol* singer, whose family was backstage:

> A stagehand offered to take them down to tour the basement. "I thought we aren't supposed to go down there," said a woman guest. "The little girl said bad things happen down there."
>
> What little girl? The woman turned around to point to her, but no child was there. Said the woman, "She was here just a second ago!"

Dig on that for a while.

A GHOST HUNTER HITS THE ROAD

Along the highways of the American Southwest, a ghost hunter drove thousands of miles. He didn't carry special equipment like electromagnetic field meters. Nope. Antonio R. Garcez brought pens and paper and a tape recorder.

Over the years, Garcez interviewed people in New Mexico, Arizona, Yosemite National Park in California, and more. Garcez's grandfather was Mescalero Apache. His grandmother was an Otomi Indian from central Mexico. Garcez, who grew up in Los Angeles, explains a bit about his boyhood on his website:

> My parents were healers who were able to draw upon the after-death sphere. As a child, I accompanied them on their frequent visits to households blemished by the misfortunes of illness or the troubles of misguided spirits. Through this personal apprenticeship, I witnessed both the positive and negative aspects of spirits.

Something you should know: Among indigenous people across the Americas, beliefs about ghosts and the supernatural vary widely. Often these stories are unique to individual groups and build on tribal traditions and experiences.

Garcez shared a true and terrifying tale that he noted was both rare and compelling. The events took place on the Tohono O'odham (TAH-HA-noh AH-tham or TAH-HA-noh AH-dahm) reservation in south central Arizona. Seventeen-year-old Yaqui student Dave War Staff was on a late-night drive from Phoenix with his cousin, Ralph. His

Antonio Garcez collects others' reports of their encounters with ghosts.

cousin lived in Sells, Arizona, in the heart of the Tohono O'odham Nation.

Dave drove in the dark of night on an empty desert highway. In the darkness they hit a javelina, a good-size piglike animal, which cracked the grille and burst a hole in the radiator of his old car. It was very early in the morning, so they popped open the hood of the car to wait for help.

In the cold desert night and sleepy, too, the boys sat on the car's trunk to stay awake. Time moved slowly. Sometime before two a.m., they heard a rustling of bushes on the roadside. In Dave's words:

Then from out of the bushes, about twenty feet away, we saw a barefoot man! I turned on my flashlight and focused the weak yellow light on him as I yelled, "Hey, what's up?" The man stopped and turned to face us . . . I thought he was a desert tramp. There are a few of those old guys living out there. Ralph yelled out, "Watch out. We hit a javelina, and it's somewhere out where you're walking!" . . . We both yelled out, "Hey, you, can't you hear us? Get away from there."

Now they started feeling scared. What was someone doing out in the desert at that hour?

The man stopped, turned in our direction, and looked at us. We were definitely on the edge at that point. I though,t if this guy has a gun, in which direction would we run? I spoke to Ralph. "This guy is some kind of weirdo. We better be careful."

Then the man took a few more steps toward the highway, and we both got a real good look at him. He was dressed in very little clothing. On his thin waist he wore a tight-fitting, dark-colored cloth that draped over one knee. Around his neck were several long necklaces with large white beads or shells. He wore his hair short with bangs above his glaring eyes. One obviously strange thing was his hair. It was greasy or wet, because when I focused the light from my flashlight on it, it shone. He was about five feet tall and very thin. He was an older man, because his face showed the signs of age.

Dave used the word *walk*, but the stranger floated a good two inches above the asphalt road, as if walking on air.

As he re-entered the brush, unlike before, we didn't hear any of the twigs breaking under his feet. Ralph and I looked at each other and jumped off the trunk, ran inside the car, and quickly locked the doors! We knew this was no tramp. It had to be a ghost! You had to be there to feel the energy to know that this was a real ghost.

Help finally arrived before dawn in the form of two artists road-tripping across the desert. Happily for Dave and his cousin, the passersby roped up their car and towed it to town.

Dave and Ralph shared their wildly weird night with Ralph's family in Sells. The older folks said the nightwalker was no stranger: It was, in fact, a ghost of an ancient Indian from the spirit world.

Dave decided he'd never again drive in the desert at night.

FACTLET

FOR YOUNG INVESTIGATORS WHO are learning about indigenous Americans, Antonio Garcez offers this advice:

- Research, personally investigate, and learn about cultures, philosophies, and spiritual traditions other than your own.
- Pop culture's views on ghosts are predominately developed for commercial consumption and entertainment. Native American views are formulated from centuries of respected cultural traditions and spirituality.
- An important point . . . keep reading, and don't accept one author's theory as the only true answer.

Research. Respect. Read. As you investigate ghosts, or anything else, remember Antonio Garcez's advice.

CHAPTER FIVE

A TREASURE TROVE OF GHOSTLY GUARDIANS

HIDDEN TREASURES. DOESN'T THAT SOUND LIKE AN invitation to adventure? Sometimes, these hidden hide-aways are guarded by—ghosts!

PIRATE TREASURES FROM COAST TO GHOST

Many pirates became ghosts, because those bad guys had better chances of getting killed than most in the 1600s and 1700s. Today, people armed with metal detectors sweep beaches, hills, and mountains looking for buried treasure along the Atlantic coastline. Thanks especially to a real pirate named William Kidd.

Perhaps you've heard of Captain Kidd. His tale is both creepy *and* true!

Born a Scotsman in about 1650, Kidd found his way to a nautical life. By age forty-five, he had made his name as a privateer across the Caribbean Sea. He caught the fancy of a well-off widow, and he made New York City his home. As a privateer, Kidd captained his own ships for Great Britain and attacked enemy vessels in the name of King William. Some were ships flying flags from enemy countries like France, while other times, Kidd took aim at actual pirates. Whatever he plundered went into the British treasury, with Kidd and his men keeping a healthy portion.

In about 1695 Kidd was licensed to privateer along the African coast and around the Cape of Good Hope to the Indian Ocean and the Red Sea. He was away for three years. But when Kidd returned to New York with his ship's hold stuffed with

Author/illustrator Howard Pyle drew a vivid image of Captain William Kidd that was published in *Howard Pyle's Book of Pirates: Fiction, Fact & Fancy Concerning the Buccaneers & Marooners of the Spanish Main,* in 1921.

gold and gemstones, he was arrested. During his long voyage, fact and fiction had swirled into a mess of accusations.

Had William Kidd the privateer turned into Willian Kidd the pirate? Many believed he had, and Kidd was seized from his family and sent to England along with his captured treasure.

It was never clear whether Kidd was guilty of piracy. He languished in prison for a year, until a court convicted him.

A drawing of William Kidd's gibbeted body, hung as a warning to would-be pirates, appeared in Charles Ellms's *The Pirates Own Book* in 1837.

He was hanged at Execution Dock on the Thames River in a spot especially set up for pirates. In fact, poor William Kidd was hanged twice. The first time, the rope broke, depositing the luckless man on the dock. So he was strung up again, and that time, the rope held firm. Kidd's body was gibbeted in a metal frame to dangle on the riverbank until it rotted away.

But did Kidd's riches go to London with him? No one could pinpoint precisely Kidd's movements during his years of privateering. Maps appeared in the bottoms of old sea chests, supposedly marking spots where Kidd and a few trusted seamen had sunk his loot. Rumors flew that he'd buried treasures all over—up and down New England's coast.

Along with those hidden jewels were planted a trove of ghost sightings. In Wethersfield on the Connecticut River, a treasure hunter claimed he met the ghost of William Moore, one of Kidd's crew whom the captain had murdered. Others say that Kidd himself haunts hidden hoards along the Connecticut River.

An old history of Northfield, Massachusetts, written in the 1800s, recounted another of these gems. It took place on Clark's Island (earlier named Field's Island) in the Connecticut River. This account reveals that the treasure hunters had to work in total silence.

Like so many places—possible and impossible—this island was reputed to be one of the spots where Captain Kidd the pirate buried a chest of gold. The legend is that Kidd and his men ascended the river— how they got over the three falls with their ponderous [very heavy] load is not stated—till they reached this secluded island. Here, having placed the heavy chest in its hole, they sacrificed by lot one of their number, and laid his body a top of the treasure, that his ghost might forever after defend it from all fortune-seekers. Many a man longed for the gold, but had not the courage to disturb the ghost. But in an evil hour, Abner Field, after consulting a noted conjurer, and ascertaining the exact spot where the chest was buried, resolved to "tempt the devil on the haunted isle." In trusting the secret to two confederates [fellow pirates]—for nothing could be done without the presence of three—he waited for the propitious time, which was when the full moon was directly over-head at midnight. They were to form a triangle around the designated point, and work in perfect silence—as a word spoken would break the charm! Having reached the island, and fixed upon the spot, they begin. The hard labor and terror of the still midnight, with its imagined dusky sprites, brought out the big drops of perspiration; but they dug with desperation, for if the cock should crow the spell would dissolve. Raising the crow-bar for a mighty stroke, down it goes—clink! against the iron lid. "You've hit it!" exclaims one, forgetting the charge of silence. Alas! for that word. The charm is broken; and instantly the chest settled down out of reach and as instantly the disturbed ghost appeared, flitting around them! And before they can collect their scattered senses, Satan himself—a full six feet tall—rises from under the bank, crosses the island "like a wheel," going right through a hay-stack, and plunges into the river with a yell and splash!

Poor Abner Field . . .

BURIED TALES OF HIDDEN TREASURE

Sometimes ghosts come and sit on your front steps, visit a while, and tell you about hidden treasure. That's what happened a long time ago to a woman in South Carolina. The woman, whose name we don't know, told her neighbor, Janie Gallman, about the visits.

Many years passed, and when Janie Gallman was an old woman she, too, had a visitor, in 1937. By now Gallman was living in an "old ladies' home" in Spartanburg, South Carolina. Her visitor, F. S. DuPre, who worked for the United States government, was there to speak with several old African American women. All had been enslaved as very young girls during the Civil War.

The visitor had grown up in the same area. DuPre (we don't know if the writer was a man or woman) took notes as the elderly women spoke.

Back in the office, DuPre typed out these notes into a written transcript. In the typewritten manuscript, DuPre referred to her/himself as "the writer."

The writer found two ex-slaves sitting on the porch passing the time of day with those who passed the house.

They both spoke very respectfully and asked me to come in. One was seated and she asked me to have a seat by her. Her name was Janie Gallman and she said she was eighty-four years of age. Upon my telling her my name she stated she knew my father and grandfather and had worked for them in days gone by.

Miss Gallman spoke of her childhood in slavery, the jump rope games she played with the overseer's children, working in her parents' garden, and the wild turkeys and hogs she saw. Then her topic changed. To ghosts. Miss Gallman said she couldn't "conjure," or call them, but she'd seen a few.

[S]he had seen ghosts two or three times. One night she saw a light waving up against a piece of furniture, then come towards her, then flicker about the room, but she wasn't able to see anybody holding the light. She had heard of headless men walking around, yet had never seen any.

A neighbor told her [Janie Gallman] a woman ghost came to her house one night, just sat on the front steps and said nothing, repeated her visits several nights in succession, but said no word as she sat on the front step.

One night the neighbor's husband asked the ghost what did she want, why she sat on the steps and said nothing. The ghost then spoke and told him to follow her . . . and she unearthed a jar of money. The woman ghost told him to take just a certain amount and to give the rest to a certain person. The ghost told the man if he didn't give the money to the person she named, she would come back and tear him apart. He very obediently took the small amount of the money and gave the balance where the ghost directed, and he never saw the woman sitting on his steps any more.

Stories like Miss Janie Gallman's of buried treasure were told in African American families for years. *Told*—not written down or printed in books—what we call an "oral tradition."

CHAPTER SIX

———◇———

FLYERS, WHISTLERS, DOLLIES, AND A MEDIUM

SOMETIMES ONE DISCOVERS GHOSTS THAT STICK IN one's mind. This chapter offers several of them. So creepy...

THE FABLED FLIGHT 401

Ghosts and their stories often rise from human tragedy. When the RMS *Titanic* sank in 1912 with the loss of 1,500 on board, there soon appeared ghostly sightings of its phantom double, its deck packed with drowned passengers.

Move forward in time and you'll uncover more ghosts rising like fog from a swamp on a winter morning. In 1974 an investigative journalist named John G. Fuller, who wrote

This Lockheed L-1011 TriStar is similar to the aircraft that crashed in Florida's Everglades in 1972.

books and magazine columns for a living, heard fresh ghost gossip. Rumors were flying that the pilots killed in a recent air disaster were haunting other air crews.

In December 1972 an Eastern Airlines jet crashed in the Florida Everglades. The flight from New York to Miami carried 163 passengers, from small babies to elderly people, plus three pilots and a crew of ten flight attendants. All were aboard a brand-new Lockheed L-1011, one of the world's first jumbo jets.

Due to a series of unexpected events, the pilots didn't notice that the altitude-hold function of the autopilot was not engaged. With the pilots trying to fix other problems, the L-1011 descended slowly and hit the ground in the swampy Everglades. Seventy-five people survived the accident. All three pilots, as well as two flight attendants, were among the 101 people lost.

Within weeks, airline employees across the industry began sharing strange tales about the doomed flight. People swapped stories that the ghosts of two dead pilots were appearing to other airline crew members at work.

John Fuller was aboard a Scandinavian Airlines flight when he first heard the story from a flight attendant. Fuller already was researching a different book. He didn't dwell on the ghosts. But a year later, when Fuller was flying on Eastern Airlines, he asked a flight attendant about the ghost reports from Flight 401.

"That's not funny," she said.

She told him she'd experienced a chilling "presence" two months after the accident when she was working in the galley on another L-1011. The flight attendant asked Fuller not to use her name, as did most of the Eastern Airlines crew members who eventually told their ghostly experiences; they feared being sent to the company psychiatrist and losing their jobs. When Fuller began to pull together bits and pieces of information, he was baffled and unnerved.

He thought about Carl Sandburg, a plainspoken American poet. "Carl Sandburg once said that death is simply part of life. If it is, it is a legitimate area to explore, even if it is difficult."

Fuller hunted for eyewitnesses, those who saw the pilots' ghosts.

(Something for you to remember: These were the days before social media and online message boards that pilots peruse. For the most part the stories were passed on from one person to another *directly*, another example of an oral tradition.)

Fuller published the entire account in *The Ghost of Flight 401* in 1976. The opening half of his book covers events leading up to the crash and its aftermath. Then there is the second half, when Fuller relates the paranormal events that followed.

In March 1973, about three months after the crash, another Eastern Airlines L-1011 aircraft was flying from New York to Fort Lauderdale. This airplane was known as #318, part of the tail number that identifies a specific aircraft under rules posted by the Federal Aviation Administration.

A pair of flight attendants, Ginny and Denise (both false names), were working in the galley. On this brand-new airplane, the galley lay in the front of the plane beneath the main floor. Two tiny elevators carried the flight attendants downstairs. There they heated passenger meals in stainless steel ovens and loaded them onto food carts. The carts went upstairs by elevator, and other flight attendants rolled the carts down the aisle to serve dinner. It was usually warm and pleasant working in a galley away from the hubbub upstairs.

Denise and Ginny were very busy going up and down to the galley. Then one time Ginny rode back down to find the galley empty. Denise had grabbed the other elevator to ride up to the passenger cabin again.

A photo of an L-1011 galley shows its side-by-side elevators linking the galley to the main deck above.

All alone now, Ginny started to sense a presence in the empty galley. She thought Denise was playing a joke on her by hiding, but nothing happened. Ginny had a growing, dreadful feeling that someone else was in the room; it "became almost intolerable."

Thinking that her friend was playing games, Ginny checked the cabinets. No Denise.

Terrified, Ginny rode upstairs. A sympathetic flight attendant took her to the back of the airplane. There stood Denise, also visibly shaken. Both had felt the same sensation while downstairs alone.

They hadn't compared notes; each had only told the third flight attendant their chilling news. Like Ginny, Denise had been "immediately hit with a cold, very clammy feeling, something she had never felt before." All three agreed to say nothing about the creepy cold to anyone.

Ginny continued to fly trips on the L-1011. A few weeks later, she boarded #318 and descended to the galley to heat meals, the usual gig. Both elevators were running slowly, and—impatiently, as people will do—she pressed the button several times. Waiting in the galley, she leaned back to rest against the plane's starboard (right) wall. In view was a door that led to a compartment with the plane's electrical equipment.

Fuller's narrative described the next eerie event:

> Out of the corner of her [Ginny's] eye, she became aware of [a] hazy cloudlike formation, just in front of the bulkhead wall, above the door. Puzzled, she turned and looked at it. The galley was brightly lighted, and she had no trouble in examining it in detail. It was not condensation or steam or smoke; she knew that. It seemed to be about the size of a grapefruit, but it was getting bigger. It was also pulsating in a strange way, and the shape was much more substantive and articulate than smoke . . .
>
> She pushed the elevator button again, and then turned back to look. The cloud was now the size of a slightly elongated basketball, a few inches out from the wall, and was beginning to form into a thicker, much more solid shape. She was fascinated, transfixed by it . . .

She pushed the elevator button harder and turned her face away. "Perhaps," she said to herself, "if I don't look at it, it might go away." She pushed the button again. The elevator still didn't come.

She wanted to look and not look at the same time. She could still see the shape out of the corner of her eye. It was more pronounced than ever . . . It was clearly forming into a face, half-solid, half-misty . . .

Just as the elevator reached the galley level, she looked again. It was a complete, clear face now, with dark hair, gray at the sides, and steel-rimmed glasses now forming clearly on the three-dimensional image. There was no question it was a face, and no question that it was wearing glasses. They were now sharp and clear.

The glasses and hair left no doubt. The apparition resembled the captain of Flight 401.

∿

Every day airline crew members ride on planes to work or return home with paying passengers. This process is called deadheading. If there's room and the flight captain agrees, pilots also may deadhead on jump seats in cockpits.

About a month after Ginny and Denise had their creeped-out experience in the galley, #318 was being prepared to fly from Newark to Miami and then return back to

Newark, a turnaround flight. Everything seemed ready to go: The second officer had finished his outdoor walk-around of the aircraft, and the captain and copilot were seated in the cockpit, running checklists. Flight attendants were boarding passengers and sending food containers downstairs to the galley.

The senior flight attendant, named Sis (again a false name), walked through the front (first class) and the back (the main cabin) of the plane, making a head count of the passengers. Her checklist was off by one, not all that unusual. Patterson did a recount, only to discover another Eastern Airlines captain sitting in first class. She spoke to him politely and asked if he would be jump-seat riding on the trip. She didn't have him on her list.

The uniformed passenger didn't reply, nor did he glance up at her. He looked straight ahead. Patterson repeated her question. "I beg your pardon, Captain. I've got to check you off either as a jump-seat or first-class-pass ride. Could you help me?"

Again there was no answer as the mute pilot looked straight ahead.

At this point the situation became a problem for the flight captain—the man in charge of the entire flight. He climbed out of his cockpit seat and came out to the first-class section. About half a dozen passengers watched. The flight captain leaned in to speak to the seated stranger. "Then he froze," Fuller wrote. The stranger was the captain of Flight 401.

At that, an inexplicable thing happened. The captain seated in first class vanished. There one minute—gone the next.

More weird stuff went down. An apparition of the second officer showed up on other flights. He had been a popular guy, and his ghost seemed helpful, too.

On one occasion, it assisted a flight attendant with a broken oven in a galley. On another flight, it deadheaded in the cockpit jump seat to warn the three-man crew of an impending electrical failure. The captain did a recheck and found a faulty circuit. Then and only then did the three crewmen do a double take. The helpful deadheader was the ghost of the Flight 401 second officer.

Theories had floated that any ghosts in L-1011 galleys could simply be reflections bouncing off the oven windows—until #318 was winging its way from New York to Mexico City. One flight attendant peeked into an oven in the galley, only to see the second officer's face looking back. She flew upstairs to grab another flight attendant, who also saw the ghost face in the oven window. They called up to the flight deck, and the flight engineer came down to take a look. That made three crew members who saw the face.

The ghost had a warning for the flight engineer. "Watch out for fire on this airplane." Eventually, two out of the aircraft's three engines failed, one during flight.

John Fuller dug into the repair records on #318. He learned that when engine number one was taken apart, mechanics couldn't see any reason for it to have malfunctioned. Moreover, for whatever reason, the cockpit voice recorder had been replaced with a different one.

Could it be that the first recorder had picked up chatter among the crew about the ghost?

ISLA DE LAS MUÑECAS–THE ISLAND OF THE DOLLS

In Xochimilco, Mexico (So-Shee-MEEL-ko), there's a bit of land surrounded by water where dolls have their day—a creepy day, to be sure! It's the Island of the Dolls, Isla de las Muñecas (EE-luh day las moon-YAY-kas). Xochimilco, an ancient city, sits amid canals that once were a lake in central Mexico.

To get there, you need a boat. Everywhere you look when you walk this eerie island, dolls greet you—or gross you out. They hang from or are nailed up in trees: heads, arms, legs, and entire figures, all in tribute to a little girl who was once found dead on the island.

Many years ago, a caretaker on the island, Julian Santana Barrera, said he discovered the child, who had seemingly drowned. When he spotted a doll afloat nearby in the canal, he fished it out and hung it from a tree. Had the dolly belonged to the little girl? The caretaker treasured the dangling doll as a symbol of respect to her spirit.

But Barrera didn't stop with one. Over time he gathered scads of dolls of all kinds, not to mention bits and pieces of some, plus the occasional stuffed animal. He strung them all over the little island. Now no matter where you turn, you get an eyeful. Their spirits beg you to cradle them. Possibly you'll get an earful, too—passersby on canal boats claim they've heard the dolls whispering to one another.

Barrera died in 2001. It was reported that he drowned in the canal. Would it surprise you to learn that he now haunts the Island of the Dolls?

Years after he died, Julian Barrera's collected dolls still hang from trees and ogle visitors with their creepy eyes.

A MEDIUM WITH BIG TALENT

Ghost movies and programs go back to your great-grand-parents' days. The most popular comedy of the 1980s, when your parents and grandparents were younger, was a film called *Ghostbusters*, staring Dan Aykroyd— a big star who did scathing comedy on TV as a member of a team of ghost hunters. (Perhaps you've seen the *Ghostbusters*' remake with an all-woman team.)

Dan Aykroyd knew ghosts; his whole family did. For four generations in Canada, the Aykroyds, especially Dan's great-grandfather Dr. Samuel Aykroyd, had ties with the paranormal. By day Dr. Aykroyd was a dentist. By night he was a spiritualist. Dr. Aykroyd and his wife, Ellen, hosted séances in their farmhouse on a lake in eastern Ontario, where friends gathered in a darkened room to watch a medium at work.

Dr. Aykroyd's favorite medium was a young fellow named Walter Ashurst. He seemed to be an ordinary guy, but as a kid he had sensed he was in touch with the spirit world. For that his father had punished him. The Aykroyds, however, welcomed Walter warmly.

Early on, Walter had tough times as a medium. During the opening twenty minutes of a séance, he'd see and describe the spirits—mostly their aches and pains, like crushed or broken bones. Then Ashurst entered a deep trance for up to an hour and a half, when he was more or less out of it and had no clue what came out of his mouth. Coming back to reality wasn't easy for him and usually led to a coughing spell.

But over the years, Ashurst grew his uncanny ability to enter a deep trance. Lights would come and go. Spirit voices, table tipping, whistling, and random lights both large and small all were signs of a successful séance. He "channeled," spoke, for the spirits of a number of distinct individuals from across space and time. There was Lee Long from the Ming dynasty in China; three indigenous spirits named Blackhawk, Broken Arrow, and Black Feather; an ancient Egyptian prince named Blue Light; a North African named Carol Andrew; and Mike Whalen, an Irishman. The spirits spoke of many things. Above all, they encouraged Aykroyd's circle to try to conjure up a ghost.

Peter H. Aykroyd, Dan's father, stumbled upon old Dr. Aykroyd's journals and notes in a blue trunk hidden in the attic of the old farmhouse. They proved to be a family

This old image, called a "spirit photo," shows Dr. Samuel Aykroyd encircled by four spirits of the dead.

treasure and provided the perfect set of primary resources for Peter H. Aykroyd to write *A History of Ghosts: The True Story of Séance's, Mediums, Ghosts, and Ghostbusters.*

Clearly, old Dr. Aykroyd and his circle of friends had hoped that a ghost figure would appear—"materialize"—during a séance. As of April 1931, that hadn't happened, but Dr. Aykroyd mentions this:

> We sat again for materialization. The medium went into a trance, then we put the lights out. He left his chair and went around to a sitter on the opposite side of the table, standing at his back and placing his hands at the back of the sitter's neck and taking one of the sitter's hands in one of his hands. Soon the sitter felt strong vibrations as if he were holding an electric battery and then dense waves of light of whitish appearance are formed right in front of him. The waves flowed up and down and formed rings with a dark band around the rings. One of the sitters saw the outline of a face forming in one of the rings of the whitish substance floating in front of this particular sitter.

The spirits seemed watchful for the sitters welfare during séances. Sometimes a group member would begin to show signs of pain or distress. In seconds, Ashurst the medium lost contact with that spirit, and another spirit, a "control," replaced it. This happened during the same meeting:

> At that moment, the sitter in front of whom the "whitish substance" had appeared began to complain that his eyes were watering and sore. The medium [Ashurst] immediately dropped his hands limply to his sides and another control took possession of him. This control explained that they had stopped "operating" on the first sitter because they were afraid they would injure him.

The "whitish substance" was said to be ectoplasm. It's strange stuff, according to Peter Aykroyd. You can't put your hands on it. It shows up in the dark or near-dark during séances, for instance—and also in "spirit" photos. Seeing ectoplasm up close was quite a reward.

But take note: when *Ghostbusters* was made in 1984, ectoplasm became green, gooey, and disgusting.

CHAPTER SEVEN

GHOSTS MAKE WAR

THESE DAYS, HIGHWAYS EVERYWHERE LEAD US TO haunted places, including battlefields where wars were fought long years ago.

APPARITIONS AT ANTIETAM IN THE AMERICAN CIVIL WAR

Historians say that the Civil War was America's bloodiest. As you go through school, see movies, or play video games, likely you will come across names of the war's famous battles, like Bull Run, Vicksburg, Shiloh, Fredericksburg, and Gettysburg.

Billows of smoke at the Battle of Antietam are like specters rising above the tragic field of war.

The war's deadliest battle took place near a little "burg" named Sharpsburg in western Maryland on September 17, 1862. The Battle of Antietam drew its name from a creek that ran through the battleground. From dawn until dusk, Union and Confederate soldiers fought with rifles and cannon fire across farmers' fields, country roads, and Antietam Creek.

A narrow, low-lying road became a bloody mess at midday:

Toward the center of General Robert E. Lee's line Confederate troops positioned themselves in an old country lane called the Sunken Road. Standing in this ready-made earthwork they mowed down the first advances of Union forces. But as the hours passed, the Federals [Union soldiers] circled the Sunken Road and the ditch became a deathtrap. Rebel soldiers fell under a rain of bullets until 2,000 Confederate dead and wounded lay in the road, known ever after as Bloody Lane.

By day's end, there were twenty-three thousand casualties—dead, wounded, or missing men. Five thousand

Bodies of the dead line Bloody Lane after the Battle of Antietam.

Alexander Gardner photographed members of the Irish Brigade, some of who fell at Antietam.

five hundred of them fell in and around Bloody Lane. The line of battle itself had barely budged. Still, General Robert E. Lee, who led the far-outnumbered Confederate Army, was able to preserve his army and fight the war for two and a half more years.

You need only lay eyes on the old battlefield, or look at photos of the dead and wounded, to sense the loss among families from both the North and South.

Antietam has its soldier ghosts, of course. Folks will tell you that "the boys" wander everywhere. Visitors have snapped photos of orbs and the like, and you can see some of these online.

Along Bloody Lane especially, visitors have claimed to see phantom soldiers. Others have witnessed a riderless horse bounding over Antietam Creek. Weird singing has rung out along the road.

Historians can actually name that eerie tune. It is an old Irish melody. The so-called Irish Brigade from New York City had fought at Bloody Lane. (This particular unit was made up of Irish Americans.) They were known to chant an old Gaelic battle tune, "Faugh-a-Balaugh" (Fah-ah-bah-lah), "Clear the Way!" The Irish Brigade lost sixty percent of its men to death or wounds in the Battle of Antietam.

GHOSTS OF LOUDOUN COUNTY

About an hour south of Antietam lies Rock Hill Cemetery in Loudoun County, Virginia. A caretaker named Vernon Peterson was passing an old grave one day, when something otherworldly got his attention. Peterson happened to glance down at an ancient grave marker to see the name of its occupant, Dennis W. Weaver, carved in stone. Beneath the name appeared the letters CO. D. 1 U.S.C.I.

"It was as if [something] grabbed me by the leg," he said. The name, carved in the shape of an arch. The mysterious letters underneath. "It got to me so much, I had to try to find out what it [all] meant."

Peterson had been taking care of the old graveyard for fifty-seven years. He'd never thought about the set of letters

carved beneath Weaver's name. "CO. D. 1 U.S.C.I." But once that chill went creeping across his leg, he decided to decode them.

Peterson embarked on a research project about Dennis Weaver. In time he connected with a local historian, Kevin D. Grigsby. That led to a book, Grigsby's *From Loudoun to Glory: The Role of African-Americans from Loudoun County in the Civil War*. Grigsby's research unearthed bushels of information.

Dennis Weaver was a Civil War veteran. Those quizzical letters under Weaver's name meant "Company D, 1st United States Colored Infantry." Weaver had served in an all-black unit of the United States Army. Grigsby dug into the background behind many more names and filled his book with facts about local African Americans who had fought for the Union.

Was it Dennis Weaver's ghost that had led Peterson to make his inquiry? Now there are stories behind the dead buried in Rock Hill Cemetery. We have solid information about fellow members of Weaver's unit named Abraham Mill, Claiborne Jackson, Gabriel C. Fields, and a sharpshooter named Julius Caesar. And there are many more who fought with other units.

What an accomplishment! Kevin Grigsby might never have written that book—except for Vernon Peterson, the elderly groundskeeper who paid attention to a feeling he couldn't quite put his hands on.

A BRITISH BOGEY ON A BELGIAN BYWAY

This book about ghosts was written *exactly* one hundred years since the end of a terrible conflict first called The Great War, now called World War I. Before we move on to its ghosts, let's take a moment to dig into a bit of history.

In August 1914 the Central Powers, the empires of Germany and Austria-Hungary, went to war against the Allies, the empires of France, Great Britain, and Russia. Due to a messy web of treaties and agreements among nations on six continents, thirty-two different countries took part. In the end the Central Powers lost the war.

Much of the fighting took place along the Western Front, a battle line that ran for more than four hundred miles (six hundred and seventy-five kilometers) from the coast of Belgium across France and into Germany.

The first battles of World War I came in September 1914, when Germany invaded Belgium, a small, neutral country. The huge numbers of dead and wounded shocked army generals and soldiers' families. Most had believed that their men would be home by Christmas.

Instead, the war dragged on for four years and killed *millions*.

It was a strange irony that England and France, now allies, had fought each other at Agincourt, France, five hundred years before. The Battle of Agincourt became legendary when William Shakespeare wrote his play *Henry V*. England won the battle thanks to its ranks of longbowmen, archers with tall bows made of springy yew wood. A longbowman could shoot an arrow well over three hundred yards (two hundred and seventy-four meters). That's the length of three football fields!

The British army first fought Germany in the Battle of Mons, in and around this Belgian town on August 23, 1914. Early on, the Brits overwhelmed the Germans, but by later that afternoon, German artillery had moved closer to the

The Angel of Mons inspired stories and songs to mark the heavenly rescue of British soldiers during World War I.

battle line and begun killing British soldiers. Technically, the Germans won the battle, but the British retreat kept many men alive to fight another day.

Something not quite earthly took place as the British retreated.

> It is in this phase of the battle, with the rain and the dark and the disorientation of fatigue, that some soldiers are said to have seen a bright light between them and the German forces advancing in their wake.

Along those ditches, roads, and tracks where the British had fought, a ghost story arose of their miraclous rescue. The brave bowmen of Agincourt were now a bright light of angelic archers who set their longbows and rained arrows on the Germans, forcing them to keep their distance from the retreating Brits.

British Brigadier General John Charteris added:

> Then there is the story of the "Angel of Mons" going through the Second Corps, of how the angel of the Lord on the traditional white horse, and clad all in white with flaming sword, faced the advancing Germans at Mons and forbade their further progress.

Nevertheless, Arthur Machen, a writer, claimed he had penned a story that was the actual source of the angel legend. He alleged that people in despair over the bloodshed of these early days of war had spread his story as truth.

Others, however, supplied their own evidence of the angel's heavenly help. Miss Phyllis Campbell, an English sister (nurse), who cared for the wounded, wrote: "Then came the torrid [hot] days of Mons, and suddenly a change in the wounded, utterly unaccountable." French soldiers had started asking their caregivers for religious medals of St. Michael the Archangel or St. Joan of Arc, France's patron saint.

When Campbell met an injured British soldier, he asked for a holy picture or medal of St. George, England's patron saint. Campbell added:

> There was an R. F. A. [Royal Field Artillery] man, wounded in the leg, sitting beside him on the floor; he saw my look of amazement, and hastened in. "It's true, sister," he said. "We all saw it. First there was a sort of a yellowish-mist like, sort of risin' before the Germans as they come to the top of the hill—come on like a solid wall they did—springing out of the earth just solid—no end to 'em! I just give up. No use fighting the whole German race, thinks I, it's all up with us. The next minute comes this funny cloud of light, and when it clears off there's a tall man with yellow hair in golden armour, on a white horse . . . and his mouth open as if he was saying, 'Come on, boys, I'll put the kybosh on the devils!' . . . Then, before you could say 'knife,' the Germans had turned, and we were after them . . ."

"Where was this?" I asked. But neither of them could tell. They had marched, fighting a rearguard action, from Mons, till St. George had appeared through the haze of light, and turned the enemy.

GALLING GHOSTS AT GALLIPOLI

When Great Britain went to war in August 1914, King George V's subjects from all over the empire signed up to fight. Among them were men from Australia and New Zealand. Their combined military forces became known as the ANZACs, the Australian and New Zealand Army Corps.

The Anzacs fought their first campaign against the Ottoman Empire, aka the Turks, who had joined forces with Germany and Austria-Hungary. The conflict lasted for

"A Voice from Anzac" also tagged "Funny thing, Bill—I keep thinking I hear men marching," reproduced in the *Melbourne Herald* on April 25, 1927.

eleven long months along the skinny Gallipoli penin-sula in Turkey, which bordered a narrow waterway, the Dardanelles. The Ottomans eventually won that battle, which they called the Battle of Çanakkale (ja-NAH-kah-lay).

Great numbers of soldiers, including Anzacs, were wounded or killed at Gallipoli. Today people in New Zealand and Australia remember them on Anzac Day, April 25.

As with Antietam and Mons, Gallipoli has its ghosts. Sydney Moseley, a journalist, wrote about the second day of fighting at Gallipoli going on around Suvla Bay in August 1915.

I hesitate to tell the story because of its entire improbability. I never intended to tell it, in fact. Only my own private diary and a friend should know. But here it is, after a week's cold reflection . . .

Lost in reflection in the wonderful wider scenery, I had overlooked the ground in my immediate neighbourhood, and I saw, not fifty yards from me, what I took to be a French soldier. He was lying in a manner suggestive of utter weariness. He seemed completely exhausted. I went to him. Upon getting nearer, I was surprised to see that the man was in khaki. I hailed him in French, but he did not reply; so, on reaching him, I shook him.

He started.

"What's the matter?" I asked in French, for his growth of beard denied any index to his nationality.

"Nothing," he replied listlessly in London French.

"Oh, you're English," I said. "What regiment? How do you come to get here? Do you want to get to the base?"

He made an effort.

"Don't ask me questions, but, if you like, listen. I'm dying. I don't know how I came here and I don't recollect what has happened. I don't want to get to the base, for it would be useless. City clerk I was, and now I'm a soldier, and glad of having seen a bit of life instead of being cooped up in an office till the end. I've never been strong, but I cheated the doctor into passing me. Never mind how. There's mother, my sister, and me. My sister didn't want me to go. Of course I had to come. 'You know what it means if you never come back,' she said. 'It would mean far worse if I didn't go,' I said. When I went she kissed me—for we were old pals but—I've never forgotten the look she gave me in parting. She seemed to know I would never return."

He suddenly raised himself on his elbows and pointed to a cluster of bushes about twenty yards away from which I had just come.

"She's over there," he said in a strained whisper which made me doubt his sanity. "The same look as she gave me at the station. You see her?" he said sharply. I put my water-bottle to his lips, but he dashed it away. "You see her?" he repeated wildly.

I made a pretence of looking. These hallucinations, I thought, were not uncommon. I had met another such case only recently. Yet I looked and started. At the spot where his trembling finger pointed was a cloud of white, which, as I watched, gradually assumed a human shape. Its outlines were not distinct, but, unless I had become afflicted even as the unfortunate man at my feet had, that efflorescent form was of a graceful girl. I watched spellbound, forgetful of all else. Then a voice shouted in triumph as my sleeve was jerked.

"See, she's smiled at me."

I turned to look at him, and he was dead.

I glanced from him quickly—for here the dead are not uncommon—but the illusion, if it were such, had vanished.

It was learned later that the soldier's sister had died at home in England, shortly before she appeared to him.

CHAPTER EIGHT

GHOSTS RIDE THE RAILS

AFTER RAILROADS FIRST ROLLED ACROSS ENGLAND IN 1825, there rose spooky tales of haunted railcars and phantom engines. Powered by hot, coal-burning stoves, the engine boiled water into steam, which in turn forced giant pistons to turn its iron wheels. There was lots of steam around steam engines, steam that could as easily be discerned as something else . . .

A PRESIDENT'S PHANTOM FUNERAL TRAIN

On April 14, 1865, President Abraham Lincoln and his wife, Mary, took a carriage from the White House to the theater. Days before, peace had come to the United States after the Civil War. But a group of Confederate assassins still plotted to kill the president and others in his cabinet.

The play had nearly finished when the actor John Wilkes Booth sneaked into the box where Lincoln and his party sat. Booth fired a small handgun and shot the president in the back of the head. Lincoln died early the next morning.

News of the assassination zipped along telegraph wires across the country. For three weeks, the nation honored the slain Lincoln. His body, covered with an American flag, lay in state first in the White House and then in the high-domed Capitol Rotunda. Thousands passed by the open casket to pay their respects.

Abraham Lincoln was laid to rest back home in Springfield, Illinois. A special train carried the body, with an honor guard, army band, and politicians to accompany it. Robert Lincoln, the president's eldest son, rode as far as Baltimore.

As did another of Lincoln's boys, who like his father, lay in a casket. Willie Lincoln, only eleven years old, had died of typhoid fever in the White House in 1862. His little coffin had rested in a mausoleum in Washington. Now the child's body, packed into a second outer coffin, traveled along with his father. On Friday morning, April 21, the train pulled out at eight sharp.

Willie Lincoln's casket accompanied that of his father. Together, they ride the ghost train till this day.

The spirit photo shows the widowed Mary Todd Lincoln with the dead president's apparition.

The funeral train passed through hundreds of American cities and towns. In big cities like Baltimore, New York, Albany, Harrisburg, Cleveland, Indianapolis, and Chicago, Lincoln's body was removed so even more mourners could pay their respects. Not until May 3 did the funeral train pull into Springfield. Father and son were interred in a vault built into a hillside in Oak Ridge Cemetery.

There are sightings aplenty of Abraham Lincoln's ghostly funeral train, the ultimate sleeper car. Ask folks who now live along that wandering route. Many will tell you that every spring, during those same April weeks, Lincoln's phantom funeral train rolls along the tracks.

A regular stop seems to be in Albany, New York, first reported in the *Albany Evening Times* on March 23, 1872—only seven years after Lincoln's death.

In 2015 a Chicago historian and blogger named Adam Selzer, with an interest in all things ghost, published the entire 1872 article from the *Albany Evening Times*. The words are creepy and delicious.

WAITING FOR THE TRAIN

Interviews with the Night Watchman—Story of the Phantom Cars

THERE IS A SUPERNATURAL side to this kind of labor, which is as wild as its excitement to the superstitious is intense. Said the leader, "I believe in spirits and ghosts. I know such things exist, and if you will come up in April I will convince you."

He then told of the phantom train that every year comes up the road, with the body of Abraham Lincoln. Regularly in the month of April about midnight, the air on the track becomes very keen and cutting. On either side it is warm and still; every watchman when he feels this air steps off the track and sits down to watch.

Soon after, the pilot engine with long black streams [either ribbon or smoke], and a band with . . . instruments playing dirges, and grinning skeletons sitting all about, will pass up noiselessly, and the very air grows black. If it is moonlight, clouds always come over the moon, and the music seems to linger as if frozen with horror.

A few moments after [that] the phantom train glides by. Flags and streamers hang about. The track ahead seems covered with a black carpet, and the wheels are draped with the same. The coffin of the murdered Lincoln is seen lying on the center of a car, and all about it, in the air, and on the train behind are vast numbers of blue-coated men, some with coffins on their backs, others leaning upon them. It seems that all the vast armies of men who died during the war are escorting the phantom train of the President.

The wind, if blowing, dies away at once, and over all the air a solemn hush, almost stifling, prevails. If a train were passing, its noise would be drowned in this silence, and the phantom train would rise over it.

Clocks and watches always stop, and when looked at are found to be from five to eight minutes behind. Everywhere on the road about the 20th of April the time of watches and trains is found suddenly behind.

THE ST. LOUIS LIGHT

One thousand four hundred and eighty miles northwest from Springfield there's a place named St. Louis. It's pronounced SAINT LEW-ee, because this St. Louis, with its First Nations and French roots, is in Saskatchewan, Canada. Nearly every night in this little town on the prairie, citizens say, a ghost train passes nearby.

They call it the St. Louis Light, but the story of this phantom is dark. Back in the 1920s, a conductor with the Canadian National Railway was hit by a passing train. The poor man lost his head. Eventually, the tracks were removed. But ever since, a glowing ball of white has hung around the old railway bed on the northern outskirts of town. None other than the St. Louis Light.

Many people state flatly that they've seen the phantom train. Some years back, Serge Gareau, who grew up in those parts, piled into his car with his wife and another couple and drove eighty miles from Saskatoon to look for the Light. It was eleven at night when they arrived.

CANADA

GHOST TRAIN / TRAIN FANTÔME ST. LOUIS, SK

The St. Louis Light earned itself a postage stamp in Canada Post's "Haunted Canada" series.

They pulled up beside the abandoned railway track in the rolling countryside just north of town, left the engine running to provide heat against the cool autumn evening, and waited.

> "We sat there for about an hour, and nothing was happening," Gareau recalls. "And then all of a sudden we saw this light. It was just like a train coming. A bright light coming at us, with a little red light towards the bottom."

The group watched for two hours and then, on impulse, did a little experiment. Gareau headed straight for the light, driving on the old road that ran along the track bed.

"We drove and drove and drove," Gareau told the website Virtual Saskatchewan. "And all of a sudden the light was gone. When we looked around, it was right behind us!"

Lots of folks have blogged about the St. Louis Light, including a young-adult-book author named Phil Campagna. Sometime around 2000 he was on a road trip and decided to look for the train.

> The place was wild in this light, kind of forlorn. It was April, and though the snow was gone, the trees were still winter bare. In short, it looked like a filming location for *The Blair Witch Project.* The sound of coyotes howling didn't exactly lighten the mood.

Campagna stopped his car and heard the sound of people arguing in the woods.

> They must have noticed my lights, because one of them emerged from the woods, arms waving. He started toward me, and I could see others fast behind.

Campagna backed his car down the gravel road rather than meet the angry strangers.

Train lights at night often appear along tracks at crossroads in the countryside, but no train ever passes.

The thought of catching that ghost on camera, however, eventually drew me back about half an hour later. I drew up to the barrier again and shut off the engine. It seemed quieter now, though down the abandoned rail line, I could now plainly see lights. Signal red they were, and back-up white.

Campagna started taking pictures of the red and white lights, when a truck with three teens in it rolled up.

They pulled up, and I rolled down my window to talk to them: "You guys looking for the light?"

"No!" one of three teens in the truck yelled back. "We were STUCK IN THE MUD IN THE WOODS!" (The pickup took off.)

I was now alone in the woods, and it was getting dark. I stared down the narrow railroad bed. The lights I'd just seen were gone—all but one, that is: a fuzzy, reddish one that seemed to grow and fade, approach but never get closer. I checked my camera for the photo I'd just taken . . . The lights of the pickup were there, all right, but so was the mystery light. (It shows up as a small double dot at the back. Actually, it was a single dot, but my hands may have been shaking a bit. From the cold, you know.)

I realized I was looking at the St. Louis Ghost Train Light!

RAILROAD BILL

America's old highways and byways have long spawned heroes and folk tales of antiheroes. Through the years, bandits and robbers have even made their way into pop culture. Maybe you've heard of some. Jesse and Frank James, Billy the Kid, and Bonnie (Parker) and Clyde (Barrow) all robbed banks and killed innocent people up and down American roads. Today, it's said that their ghosts haunt their family homes, buildings they robbed, and even a getaway car.

Alabama has its very own train-robbing ghost who wanders the rails of the former Louisville and Nashville Railroad from Tennessee to Florida. Legend says that the robber, a modern-day Robin Hood, was one Morris Slater, nicknamed "Railroad Bill," who made headlines from 1895 until he was shot in March 1896. Slater was a biracial man living in the segregated South.

"Railroad Bill threw boxes of food to homes alongside the track," said Don Sales, a local historian. "People would hide him—until he shot the sheriff."

Train robbery wasn't taken lightly by the men who ran railroads, and Bill was hunted up and down the trails of iron rails. Legends arose that Bill could shape-shift into a dog or other creature to elude his hunters and frighten *their* dogs—or that, in dog form, he could even join in the hunt!

Bill outfoxed the law, as well:

So the sheriff decided Railroad Bill must be hiding under the low bushes in the clearing, and he began looking around. Pretty soon he startled a little red fox that lit out through the woods. The sheriff let go with both barrels of his shotgun, but he missed. After the second shot the little red fox turned about and laughed at him—a high, wild, hearty laugh—and the sheriff recognized it. That little fox was Railroad Bill.

When a $500 reward was posted for his capture, lots of men turned up to hunt him down. The reward got bigger, up to more than twelve hundred dollars. Word got around that only a silver bullet could kill Railroad Bill.

Fate and lead bullets caught up with Morris Slater, and he was shot, legendarily eating cheese and crackers, in a general store in Atmore, Alabama, in 1896. As his embalmed corpse made its way by rail to Pensacola, Florida, folks both black and white posed to have their pictures taken with it.

"All the people believed that he was magical and mystical and a shape-shifter—they didn't believe that he could be killed, and that's why they paraded his image," Sales explained.

At the time, and using an old term for African American, an observer noted:

> One negro woman made a great speech, warning all the other negroes to not follow the steps that "Railroad Bill" had followed because it had been shown conclusively that a life of that kind would come to a bad end and that the ordinary lead bullet would kill a negro desperado as easily as would a silver bullet.

Hero or villain, Railroad Bill was memorialized in ballads early in the 1900s. You can find a few on the web. His ghost, people say, walks the tracks of the L&N Railroad. Bill also haunts St. John's Cemetery in Pensacola, where he was laid to rest in an unmarked grave.

MORRIS SLATER

"RAILROAD BILL"

DIED MARCH 7, 1896

The family of a man who wrote a book about Railroad Bill later placed a marker on the outlaw's grave.

THE SILVERPILEN OF STOCKHOLM

The citizens of Stockholm, Sweden's capital city, had been riding green-painted cars on its subway for years before the city updated its fleet. In 1966 eight sleek, shiny, unpainted aluminum subway cars (C5s) rolled onto the tracks. Quickly, the locals nicknamed the train the *Silverpilen*, "Silver Arrow." Just as fast, creepy stories about the Silverpilen circulated around the city. It seemed that once one boarded the Silverpilen, you just "traveled and traveled and traveled" and never got off.

By 1986 Bengt af Klintberg, a scholar, wrote about the silver subway train in a book:

[I]t is only seen after midnight. It stops only once every year. The passengers in the train seem to be living dead, with expressionless, vacant looks. A very common detail is that a person who just wanted to travel to the next station remained seated for one week in the Silverpilen.

Hmm . . . Plan a quick trip on one of Stockholm's silver subway cars and ride with skeletons for a week?

Stockholm has a "ghost station" at Kymlinge (KIM-ling-uh), a subway stop built in a forest of birch trees in the mid-1970s. It never opened. That unused station became the perfect stop for a ghostly subway car.

"I would say the legend about Silverpilen is very much alive today. Even though the Transport Museum does

Standard aluminum subway cars morphed into Stockholm's spooky Silverpilen.

A high-speed train passes through the lonely Kymlynge Station, never put in service. It has been home to ghost sightings through the years.

not have any C5 cars in our collection, we do occasionally get inquiries and requests about [the train] from visitors, researchers, film teams, etcetera."

Johanna Bergström of the Stockholm Transport Museum should know. She recalls:

> The story when I was growing up in the 1990s was about a young woman who got on Silverpilen late one night when she had missed the last regular train. She was suspicious to find that the train was silver in color rather than green or blue, but she saw other passengers sitting inside and boarded the train despite her suspicions.

Once it started moving, she noticed it did not stop at any of the stations; the train was speeding up rather than slowing down. When her station swiftly passed outside the window, she started panicking and looked around at the other passengers. She then discovered that they were not normal commuters. They were very still and quiet, with faces sunken with hollow cheeks, and where their eyes should be were nothing but big black holes in the skull.

She felt her panic rising as she frantically ran up and down the train to find a way off, when the train finally slowed down. The other eerie-looking passengers started moving and got to their feet. When the train stopped, she followed them out the doors to what she found to be an unfinished platform with no escalators, lighting, or even paint on the walls. Where the escalators should have been there was a solid wall, and she watched in horror as the other passengers walked right through it.

The young woman was found among the birches of Kymlinge the next morning, confused and in shock.

CHAPTER NINE

HAUNTS IN RED SPACES

BEFORE WE BEGIN, HERE ARE QUICK FACTS TO HELP YOU digest the first part of this chapter, which is about Russia:

- Russia is the world's largest country. It extends five thousand seven hundred miles (nine thousand one hundred seventy-three meters) from the Baltic Sea to the Pacific Ocean. That's eleven time zones.
- Moscow became Russia's capital city in 1918. Before then, St. Petersburg was its capital. From 1914 until 1918, St. Petersburg was called Petrograd. In 1924 Petrograd was renamed Leningrad. (You'll figure out why when you read what follows.)

● Until the Russian Revolution in 1917, Russia was called Russia. The imperial Romanov family of tsars (kings) and tsarinas (queens) ruled the kingdom until the revolution. In November 1918 a revolutionary named Vladimir Lenin and his Bolshevik Party rose to power. Eventually the Bolsheviks renamed themselves Communists. Their symbol, a red star, inspired their popular nickname: the Reds.

● In 1922 Russia's Communist government annexed a number of other countries and renamed itself the Union of Soviet Socialist Republics, or simply the USSR. The Communist Party ran the nation as a totalitarian dictatorship until the mid-1950s. After the Soviet Union fell apart in 1991, much of it again became Russia. Other parts became independent nations.

Now we turn to a ghost sighting from a longtime Russian news outlet:

Following is a condensed version of ethereal events as reported by Pravda.ru, a Russian news website, in 2006.

IN MOSCOW ON OCTOBER 19, 1923, as the autumn nights grew ever darker, a duty officer in the Kremlin noticed something strange. A bearded man was walking through the halls of the building. Not any bearded man, but the very leader of the brand-new Union of Soviet Socialist Republics, Vladimir Lenin. All by himself.

The officer made a phone call to ask for an answer: Why had Lenin shown up at work, at night, without an escort? Something wasn't right. Such a security violation was unthinkable!

As the alert security officer well knew, Lenin should have been at his home in the village of Gorki. Lenin had already survived an assassination attempt and still had bullets in his neck to prove it. But those in the know—and these were only a handful of Soviet bosses—knew that Lenin was not a well man.

Partly paralyzed in one arm and leg, the bearded, balding Lenin hobbled and used a walking stick. These days, the fifty-three-year-old stayed close to home with his wife, Nadezhda Krupskaya. However, the unannounced visitor at the Kremlin walked straight up and stick free.

Apparently, an apparition of the Soviet leader was taking a walk down memory lane. Lenin's presumed ghost climbed the steps to visit his old apartment and study before he dropped by the meeting rooms of the Council of People's Commissars, the government. He finished his walking tour by cruising on foot through the Kremlin courtyard.

All this was vouched for by a group of military cadets who saluted Comrade Lenin, as they would have called him, outdoors in Red Square. From all appearances, Lenin was having a fine time.

Vladimir Lenin, pictured in a Russian propaganda poster, was a larger-than-life figure to his people during the days of the Union of Soviet Socialist Republics.

Could a ghost actually hang out in an office while his mortal self was still alive? We can wonder. A man couldn't be in two places at once, and Lenin's Communist Party comrades, officially atheists, didn't believe in ghosts. So Soviet officials made up fake news: a report that Lenin had paid a visit to Moscow on October 19.

Vladimir Lenin died at home in Gorki three months later, on January 21, 1924, at the age of fifty-three.

Lenin's ghost continued to appear. A second historian told a reporter his story. One day, he recalled, he'd been introduced to an older man at lunch. This gray-haired fellow had been a high-ranking colonel in the KGB, the notorious Soviet spy agency. He was in charge of security for the very building that housed Lenin's old apartment and study.

The lunch chat came around to ghosts, and then the KGB man stopped smiling. He stated that his coworkers had often heard sounds of footsteps and more in Lenin's old stomping grounds. Noises like the scraping of furniture legs on the floor. Of course, the colonel stressed, the rooms were both locked and sealed.

When Russian president Boris Yeltsin took office in the early 1990s, he set up shop in that building. His chief of staff, Sergei Filatov, got creeped out by strange noises coming from right above his office. And where was the dedicated chief of staff working so late at night? Directly under Vladimir Lenin's very own apartment.

FACTLET

TSAR NICHOLAS II

A QUESTION LINGERS ABOUT Lenin's actions after the Russian Revolution. Did he order the execution of Russia's Tsar Nicholas II?

In March 1917 Tsar Nicholas was forced to abdicate—give up—his right to rule Russia. The Russian monarchy, the Romanov family, had reigned for three hundred years. The new provisional government banished Nicholas, his wife, Alexandra, and their five children to far-off Yekaterinburg, Siberia.

Another revolution in November 1917 transformed Russia for the next seventy-two years. Lenin and his radical political party, the Bolsheviks, seized control. The Bolsheviks imposed a new government, the Union of Soviet Socialist Republics. Lenin stood at the top.

The entire family of Tsar Nicholas II, the last emperor of Russia, was murdered by the Communist government in 1918 after it came to power.

When his opponents fought back, his government launched a "Red Terror" crackdown and marshaled their secret police, the *Cheka*. Lenin and his Communist comrades ordered murders, many of them. Among their victims were the Romanovs. Father, mother, four daughters, a son, and some of their servants were herded into a basement in the middle of the night and executed by gunfire. Most scholars agree that Lenin ordered the killings, though nothing in writing ever came to light.

That grisly murder of a royal family took place more than a century ago. Their ghosts, or at least the ghost of the head of the family, were said to haunt that awful house in Yekaterinburg before it was demolished. Today, dressed in black, Empress Alexandra's ghost strolls the site of the old family palace in Pushkin, Russia, outside St. Petersburg.

What's more, Prince Michael of Greece, an older man who blogs about the arts, posted what he'd heard at dinner in St. Petersburg in about 1990. It seems that every single guard in the tsar's old palace, now a museum, refused to guard a particular servants' staircase. And why? They'd seen a ghost there of a small man in military uniform, his chest laden with medals. He floated in through a wall, dropped down one floor, and then floated out.

The frightened soldiers didn't know their own history very well, or they could have guessed what their officers felt sure *they* knew. The men had described Tsar Nicholas II. Perfectly.

We can wonder why the ghost of the murdered tsar doesn't show up in Lenin's apartment to take his revenge.

England's King Charles I was beheaded in front of a crowd outside his London palace.

GHOST AT THE RED LION (LONDON)

In London, England, there lies a bit of land called Red Lion Square. A ghost roams about the spot. He's reputedly the specter of Oliver Cromwell.

Oliver who? He's a huge name in England's history, because Oliver Cromwell toppled a king from his throne.

You may have heard about the American Civil War. Unless you live in the United Kingdom or Commonwealth countries, likely you haven't learned about the English Civil Wars, fought from 1642 to 1651.

Despite its small size England has a great big history and a long-lived monarchy. Rulers came and went: kings with names like Edward, John, Richard, Henry, and George, as well as queens named Mary, Elizabeth, and Anne.

In 1625 King Charles I took England's throne. Charles I believed in the divine right of kings, which meant that God had granted him permission to rule as he wished. He ruled with a heavy hand. Times were tense. All across Europe, Catholics and Protestants fought brutal wars of religion. In England, they didn't like one another, either.

Charles was both king and head of the Church of England, which was Protestant. Nevertheless, many of its traditions looked back to the days when England was a Catholic country. King Charles liked things that way.

In the 1630s there arose an angry faction of Englishmen who bitterly disagreed with how Charles ruled England. They called themselves Parliamentarians because they sat in Parliament, the lawmaking branch of government. They resisted when Charles wanted to make wars or levy taxes they didn't like.

Many Parliamentarians were Puritans, Protestants who planned to "purify" the Church of England of its Catholic rituals. Among the Puritans was one Oliver Cromwell, a strong-willed general.

Eventually, events in England, Scotland, and Ireland led to three civil wars against the monarchy. King Charles, backed by his "Cavaliers" with long flowing hair, battled the Parliamentarians. These rebels, the "Roundheads," wore short-cut hair. Among the generals in the rebel army was the very same Oliver Cromwell.

In the end King Charles lost the war and his life. He stood trial in front of Parliament members—army officers, clergy, civilians, and, notably, *not many* nobles. They found Charles guilty of treason, "a tyrant, traitor, murderer, and public enemy." Three days later, the king stepped through a window of his palace onto a scaffold. There he was beheaded.

In place of a king, a Lord Protector would rule England, and this man was none other than Oliver Cromwell. Cromwell ruled for five years and forced new laws on England's people. Protestants could worship as they pleased, Catholics had to go into hiding, and Jews, driven out of England three hundred years before, returned. Cromwell ruled as a military dictator.

Cromwell died in 1658. Quickly, monarchy returned to England. Prince Charles Stuart, son of the executed king, was anointed King Charles II.

Following a formal vote in Parliament, the king's men marched into Westminster Abbey, London's grand church that housed tombs of kings and queens. They yanked Oliver Cromwell's corpse from its coffin and spirited it to Red Lion Square a few miles north. For one night, Cromwell's body lay in a tavern called the Red Lion.

The next day, the king's men held a posthumous trial for Cromwell. He was found guilty of treason. As with Captain Kidd, Cromwell's body was gibbeted in a metal frame. At day's end, it was cut down. Then Cromwell's corpse was—beheaded.

Cromwell's head, like that of any traitor, was plopped onto a sharp spike and displayed on the roof of Westminster

Hall. The rest of his body was buried near the execution ground close to Marble Arch, a London landmark.

Or was it? Some say that loyal Roundheads kidnapped Cromwell's corpse and buried it behind the Red Lion. Centuries have passed, and layers of dirt and old buildings have piled up there since.

Now Cromwell's ghost wanders Red Lion Square and lots of spots around England, including his home in Ely. Ely's local newspaper, for one, reported that Cromwell's ghost has untied people's shoes on occasion, repeating itself after its targets have tied them back up! Alan Murdie, a British lawyer who researches ghosts, also reported on the sightings. In 1979 a woman who was a guest in Cromwell's former home sensed a male presence in a bedroom.

> She felt her arms clenched in a strong masculine grip and saw [that] the features of the room had changed. The lady did not feel any fear but rather a strong mental bond with the unseen presence and she sensed the words "It is not my way" being repeatedly spoken. The next morning red marks were visible on her arms, seen by both her husband and the [clergyman] with whom the couple had been staying.

Cromwell's ghost also haunts the grounds of Basing House, a grand, castle-like estate. The king's men defended it for three years during the civil war—until Cromwell arrived with cannons and blew it apart. There was little mercy for the Royalists inside. Only an old barn withstood the attack. Today Cromwell's ghost grandly strolls from there to empty grass where only the outline of the once-great Basing House now exists.

Then there's King Charles I, whose headless specter also has graced various places. It debuted in 1645 at the funeral of Colonel Nathaniel Stephens, a politician with another grand home, Chavenage House. Stephens, a "mild man," had had his doubts about regicide (king-killing) and had to be persuaded to side with his fellow politicians.

His daughter, Abigail, had been away . . . Returning shortly after the New year [*sic*] she was furious at her

The *Plundering of Basing House* by Charles Landseer, exhibited in 1836. A romanticized depiction of Oliver Cromwell's forces who attacked Basing House, once the grandest home in England, and burned it to the ground, killing many of its occupants.

father for bringing the family name into such disrepute, and in her anger she placed a curse upon him.

Soon afterwards Colonel Stephens was taken terminally ill.

The servants reported a mysterious black horse-drawn carriage driven by a head-less coachman pulling into the drive. The dead Nathaniel's body was seen to drift downstairs and out of the front door and into the awaiting coach. As it went its headless coachman assumed the shape of the martyr King Charles 1st—this being seen as retribution for the Colonel's disloyalty to his monarch. The coach burst into flames on passing through the manor gates.

And what about Cromwell's severed head? It has its own history, too. Word on the London streets was that a storm took down the skull and a guard sneaked it away. Bought and sold like a prize basketball, the skull passed through many quarters and even appeared in a freak show at one point. It landed in the hands of Dr. Horace N. S. Wilkinson, a loyal alum of Sidney Sussex College at Cambridge University. Cromwell had attended college there.

"Cromwell's head passed into the hands of the Wilkinson family about 1814, when it was purchased by Josiah Henry Wilkinson, who used to display it at breakfast parties," explains Nicholas Rogers, the college archivist. "Canon

The family of Dr. Horace N. S. Wilkinson (right, holding skull), aquired Oliver Cromwell's skull, which his ancestors had enjoyed showing at parties and to schoolkids.

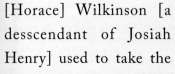
[Horace] Wilkinson [a desscendant of Josiah Henry] used to take the head to show to school-children in Woodbridge."

Dr. Wilkinson donated the skull to his alma mater. There's no official word on where Cromwell's head is secreted away at Sidney Sussex. But we do know that it's encased in a biscuit (cookie) tin to help protect the Lord Protector's head.

A RED LION IN THE WINDY CITY

Fast-forward three hundred and twenty-four years and nine hours of flying time from London, England, to Chicago, Illinois. In 1984 an Englishman named John Cordwell was breakfasting in a neighborhood known as Lincoln Park.

The Red Lion Pub in Chicago, home to several haints, underwent renovations until it finally was torn down in 2014.

(Need you wonder why? After all, Illinois's nickname is Land of Lincoln.)

Cordwell, a World War II pilot who had flown for the Royal Air Force, had emigrated from England in the 1950s. Now an architect, Cordwell's gaze fell on a ramshackle building across the street. It was a classic Chicago three-flat named Dirty Dan's, with a business on the ground floor and two floors above for apartments. Cordwell bought the building and transformed it into a classic English pub, a place for people to enjoy food and drink and swap ideas.

The old space at 2446 North Lincoln Avenue had a loooong history of haunts. Patrons at Dirty Dan's had spoken of this or that ghost over the years, including a cowboy. Best remembered was the ghost of a young woman who had died of measles in her upstairs room in 1959. There weren't vaccines to prevent measles back then, and sometimes measles killed people.

By 2008 the Red Lion was in dreadful shape, "being held up by termites holding hands," said John Cordwell's son Colin. So it was torn down. The lot sat empty for more than five years until Colin Cordwell built a spanking-new Red Lion Pub. But would its customers come back? And what about its ghosts?

They all returned—humans and haints. You can book a tour to meet a few. Dinner is included.

FACTLET

A GREAT ESCAPE

JOHN CORDWELL HAD QUITE the story. He was a pilot, psychic, and co-architect of the Great Escape. Born a Brit, Cordwell had flown as a pilot for the Royal Air Force in World War II. The story goes that at age twenty-one he realized he could see otherworldly things. Cordwell flew missions until his luck ran bad and he was shot down.

John Cordwell (*left*) and his fellow prisoners of war planned the "Great Escape" from a German prisoner-of-war camp during World War II. "The photo in the room they shared at Stalag Luft III shows John Cordwell standing on the left with my father, Arthur John Garwell, seated next to him and holding a cigarette . . . They were best friends," wrote Garwell's son John in an email to the author.

A staircase in the newly rebuilt Red Lion Pub leads to a cozy upstairs where ghosts have been sighted.

John Cordwell ended up a war prisoner, housed in Stalag Luft III, a camp in Poland. He had a lead role in planning and executing an escape of seventy-three prisoners from the camp in 1944. He didn't get a chance to flee—a fortunate break, because the Germans executed fifty of the escapees. Only three made it to freedom.

Later, Hollywood memorialized this daring plan in a huge hit film, *The Great Escape*. One of its actors, Donald Pleasence, played a role based on . . . John Cordwell! Ask your grandparents about actor Steve McQueen's motorcycle chase in the same film.

When this author dropped by the Red Lion, Colin Cordwell mentioned that his dad has apparently stuck around the Red Lion. It seems that the elder Cordwell's spirit likes to photobomb pictures taken by patrons in the pub!

CHAPTER TEN

GHOSTS SET SAIL

FOUR HUNDRED YEARS AGO, SHIPS OF WOOD POWERED by wind in their sails left Europe's ports to trade around the globe. For those bound for Asia, there was no Suez Canal to link the Mediterranean Sea to the Indian Ocean. Instead, sea captains charted their course along Africa's west coast and then east around the Cape of Good Hope in what's now the nation of South Africa.

But the Cape of Good Hope became the Cape of Bad Luck for some. Stories rose that a certain Dutch trading ship, its hold full of pricey spices and other goods on a return trip home, ran into storms there. Its captain, one Hendrick Van der Decken, swore he'd bring his ship around the cape at any cost, even if that meant sailing until doomsday. For Van der Decken and his hapless crew, that's exactly what happened. The men and ship were lost at sea, but their ghostly remains became the *Flying Dutchman*.

If you read through old yarns dating back to the 1700s, you'll find a boatload about this vicious vessel. The *Flying Dutchman* has made its appearance in paintings, books, poems, films, cartoons, anime, and a famous opera of the same name.

Many have seen the ghost ship with their own eyes. In 1881 two were British princes, Prince George and his older brother, Prince Albert Victor, who sailed with the British navy. They were the teenage grandsons of Queen Victoria of England. At that time, Albert was second in line to the throne after their father, Edward, Prince of Wales, who went on to become King Edward VII.

Albert and George were midshipmen, training as officers in Her Majesty's

A page from *The Cruise of Her Majesty's Ship "Bacchante,"* 1879–1882, showed readers the *Bacchante* at full sail.

Royal Navy. (That would be their grandmother's navy, BTW.)

The brothers' ship, the HMS *Bacchante*, sailed from England in late 1879. During its three-year voyage, it docked for a long stay at Melbourne, Australia, on the south coast. There the young princes were wined and dined and danced late into the night. When it came time to depart for Sydney on Australia's east coast, the *Bacchante* stayed behind for repairs, so Albert and George boarded HMS *Inconstant*. The brothers kept journals, notebooks, and letters about their voyage, which their tutor, John Neale Dalton, compiled into a huge book. We can wonder which prince wrote thus:

1881. WE MEET THE *FLYING DUTCHMAN*.

July 10th.–A fine day, but going very slowly, no wind. At divisions on Sunday in the flagship the midshipmen have to wear tailcoats and dirks [Scottish daggers]. Had the usual [church] service, but the men do not sing so well as in the *Bacchante*. Towards evening we are nearly becalmed.

July 11th.–At 4 A.M. the *Flying Dutchman* crossed our bows. A strange red light as of a phantom ship all aglow, in the midst of which light the masts, spars, and sails of a brig 200 yards distant stood out in strong relief as she came up on the port bow. The look-out man on the forecastle reported her as close on the port bow, where also the officer of the watch from the bridge clearly saw her, as did also the quarterdeck midshipman . . . Thirteen persons altogether saw her, but whether it was *Van Diemen* or the *Flying Dutchman* or who else must remain unknown . . .

The *Tourmaline* and *Cleopatra*, who were sailing on our starboard bow, flashed to ask whether we had seen the strange red light.

Then the story turned even darker.

At 6.15 A.M. observed land (Mount Diana) to the north-east. At 10.45 A.M. the ordinary seaman who had this morning reported the *Flying Dutchman* fell from the fore topmast crosstrees on to the topgallant forecastle and was smashed to atoms. At 4.15 P.M. after quarters we hove to with the headyards aback, and he was buried in the sea. He was a smart royal yardman, and one of the most promising young hands in the ship, and every one feels quite sad at his loss.

The Princes George and Albert witnessed both the *Flying Dutchman* and a fatal accident that day. Albert, only a little

The royal princes Albert Victor (center left) and George (center right) laid their own eyes on the *Flying Dutchman* as they trained with Great Britain's Royal Navy.

older than George, should have become king, but in 1892 he died from influenza at the age of twenty-eight. George went on to be crowned King George V in 1910.

A STRAIGHT STORY ABOUT A GHOSTLY STRAIT

Canada's Prince Edward Island is home to Anne of Green Gables, a popular character in a novel of the same name that has entertained readers for more than one hundred years. The island, however, is a very real place, a province off the coast of New Brunswick and Nova Scotia in northeastern Canada. Between them lies Northumberland Strait—a narrow body of water. The straight story is that ghost ships sail there.

> Over and over, people on both sides of the strait have seen a three-masted sailing ship on fire. Some have taken boats to try a rescue of the doomed ship, only to watch it disappear—

According to Canada Post, the nation's postal service, "Hundreds of shipwrecks have been located in the Strait, with estimates that perhaps just as many may lie below undiscovered. Whether the ships were sunk by bad weather, poor conditions or fire, the strait has become the watery grave for hundreds, possibly even thousands, of seafarers." Perfect conditions for a ghost or two!

Canada Post issued a stamp to commemorate the ghostly strait. It seems that nearby residents have seen a burning ship there for two hundred years! In 1900 some sailors in Charlottetown Harbour spotted the blazing boat and set out to rescue whomever they could, only to draw near and watch the ship vaporize in the mist. The same phenomenon happened in 2008, when a seventeen-year-old visitor to Tatamagouche Bay, a village on the other side of the strait, spotted the ship in the dead of winter. Mathieu Giguere told a local newspaper, "It was bright white and gold and looked like a schooner with three masts ..."

A local historian chatted with Mathieu about his experience. Their conversation confirmed what the historian already knew about the phantom vessel. Mathieu, like others who'd seen the burning vessel, reported that the ghost ship had three masts.

Canada Post added the burning ship of the Northumberland Strait to its spirited series of Canadian ghosts.

CANADA

PHANTOM SHIPS / NAVIRES FANTÔMES, NS / PE

CHAPTER ELEVEN

HOT SUMMERS, CHILLING GHOSTS

SUMMERTIME MEANS GHOST VISITS ACROSS ASIAN lands in China, Japan, Korea, and beyond. But they are nothing like the Western celebrations of Halloween on October 31, which are rooted in ancient Celtic beliefs from northwestern Europe. Instead, ghost traditions in Asia have their roots in two ancient religions, Buddhism and Taoism, mixed together with local customs.

For many centuries people have honored their ancestors in ways that many with European ancestors have not. The young hold great respect for the old. They believe that one's ancestors have moved on to an afterlife. These ancestors, though they may be dead, still hold power over the lives of

Chinese living in Malaysia celebrate the summer Ghost Festival by burning paper images in the nighttime streets.

the living. Therefore, when someone dies, the family honors the body with a funeral, buries it with care and respect, and forever venerates the dead one's spirit.

Once these honored dead are settled in comfort in a happy afterworld, they will bless the living: if—and it's a big *if*—their living family continues to honor them. There's an agreement. Reciprocity. The living say to the dead, "I take care of you. And *you* take care of me!"

But what to do about the unhappy ones, the angry dead? There are plenty of these "dearly departed." Perhaps the family neglected the dead one with too fast a burial—or neglected the dead one's grave thereafter. Maybe the family line stopped at some point when no new babies arrived, leaving no one to tend to the dead. Or perhaps there was no grave at all, if someone died in a shipwreck, for example. No grave? That would leave the victim's spirit at sea, likely to return as an angry ghost.

In places like China, Singapore, and Thailand, gates to the underworld swing open every summer, about halfway through the seventh lunar month in July or August. The unsettled dead wander about for the thirty days of Ghost Month (鬼月 in Chinese), out to do mischief or worse. To calm them, cities and towns hold Ghost Festivals. In the very hot and very sticky climate that's an Asian summer, the chill of a ghost celebration can cool things down for the living and the dead.

Few people want to be caught outside late at night, because a ghost might be ready to pounce. Though it's the hottest time of year, many refuse to go swimming: Ghosts await them in the water, ready to drown unsuspecting victims. Whistling? Don't do it; you might call out a ghost!

People don't buy or rent new homes; it's an unlucky time to do so.

What they *can* do during Ghost Month is visit and tidy up family grave sites and leave small gifts of food along the road for ghosts to enjoy. They also burn plenty of offerings made of paper. Paper, the perfect substitute for real, earthly stuff. For ages the Chinese have burned fake paper money to appease unhappy ghosts. In modern times paper likenesses of—yes, money—but also effigies of high-end cars, fancy homes, and even cell phones and iPads are tossed into flames.

HUNGRY GHOSTS

Of all the reports surrounding these unhappy creatures, one tops the bestseller list. It's the "hungry ghost," who once lived a greedy, ungrateful life. With huge stomachs and skinny necks, they can never be pleased.

One hungry ghost report is two thousand years old and came from India as the Buddhist religion spread across Asia. A young monk named Mulian (moo-lee-IN) followed the Buddha, a very wise and gentle man known to his believers as the Enlightened One.

The well-off young Mulian lived with his father and mother in a household of great comfort. His parents raised him to expect that he would, like his father, take a wife and have children to continue the family line. Mulian and his

In this Japanese Kyoto Ghost Scroll from the late 1100s, Mulian meets his mother, a thin-necked hungry ghost, in hell.

family would honor their ancestors, especially his own parents after they died.

Nevertheless, Mulian sensed in his own being that he wanted something different for his life. His soul needed more nourishment than easy living with his parents could offer. He shaved his head, left home, and became a follower of the Buddha. As a Buddhist monk, Mulian embarked on the path to find enlightenment.

Mulian chose a plain, simple life. He rejected riches and lived a life of little food and long days of contemplation—and no chance of falling in love or marrying, which meant no children to honor him once he'd left this world for the next.

Yet Mulian wished to fulfill his duties to his own parents after they died, to please their spirits. He especially wanted to bring offerings to his mother's spirit, who was in hell. This ancient view of hell is not a home to a devil with horns and a pitchfork but is a hell as a variety of punishments: beatings, burns from hot copper pillars, starvation, and more.

Before Mulian had left his parents' house, he'd gone away to do business in another town. He handed his mother money for her to give to the poor while he was gone. But Mulian's mother, a greedy woman, kept the money for herself.

And when she died, her soul fell into a hellish place, because she had done evil things. Her soul would spend many days there to pay for her sins.

For the time until she could pay her debt, Mulian's mother became a hungry ghost, her neck stretched so thin that she could not swallow. Mulian had to beg the Buddha to release her.

KOREA'S ANGRY GHOSTS

Lots of different ghosts haunt the Korean Peninsula; angry ones especially have appeared in literature for years. Ran Lee, an American physical therapist who was born in Korea, explains that "when souls go to the afterlife, some have *han*. When they die they have unmet needs, and these souls become angry ghosts."

Many Korean ghosts are unhappy young women who never married, the Cheonyeo Gwishin (처녀귀신 CHAW-nyuh GWEE-shin). In Korea's ancient times, women had little control over their lives. It was a girl's duty in life to serve the men in her family: first her father and his family, then her husband and his family, and finally, her sons and their families. A married woman was very reserved and always wore her hair up. But if a girl died unmarried, she had failed in her duty. She became an angry ghost, a terrorizing figure with flowing black hair and the white dress of death.

Sometimes unmarried men met the same fate after they died and became Mongdaal Gwishin (몽달귀신 MONG-dahl GWEE-shin). Their living relatives would worry that their beloved sons would morph into angry ghosts. To guarantee a different outcome, families visited their local shamans. They pled with these holy men to find a ghostly bride for their sons and arrange a marriage. Today we could say that this would be a marriage made in heaven ☺.

Nearly as haunting is a Mul Gwishin (물귀신 MOOL GWEE-shin), a water ghost. Water ghosts grab you while you swim and drown you. In the Korean language, Mul Gwishin translates as "water ghost tactics." In other words, *mul gwishin* means that someone is dragging you down to suffer along with them, a form of sabotage. It's something like the "I'm taking you down with me" expression.

Korea's scariest ghost resembles an egg.

You read that correctly. Dalgyal Gwishin ((달걀귀신 DAL-gyal GWEE-shin) is a ghost with no features. Imagine that: no eyes, nose, or mouth. No particular shape at all, just a lump of something deadly. But if you hike into Korea's mountains and happen to meet Dalgyal Gwishin on the trail, you will surely die.

A JAPANESE LESSON ON GHOSTS

You will come across several Japanese names in the coming paragraphs. Here's a basic way to pronounce them. Japanese names have many syllables. For instance, Japan's top three ghosts are Oiwa (O-I-WA), Otsuyu (O-TSU-YU), and Okiku (O-KEY-KOO). The samurai—knight—in Okiku's story is Aoyama (AH-O-YA-MA).

The island nation of Japan is fraught with ghosts. These are called yūrei (YOO-ree). But you should understand that yūrei are not the same as ghosts you see in America, Europe, or Africa.

Yūrei are specifically Japanese, tied to Japan's people in ways that most Westerners don't understand at first glance. "Yūrei," wrote Zack Davisson, "follow certain rules, obey certain laws . . . bound by centuries of culture and tradition."

Otsuyu, attended by her maid who lit their way, paid nightly visits to her lover.

Davisson should know. An American scholar of Japanese folklore, he and his Japanese wife, Miyuki, moved into a low-rent apartment in Osaka, Japan. Soon enough the young couple discovered why it was so cheap. A ghost, a *yūrei*, haunted the place, which explained the red hand- and foot-prints on the ceiling and Miyuki's night of terror when she felt herself being "slowly dragged up to a giant sucking black hole in the ceiling …"

There are huge numbers of ghosts in Japan. The top three are all women. There's Oiwa, the ghost of a real woman tracing back to the 1600s; she first appeared in Japanese writings in 1825 and can travel from spot to spot.

Then there's Otsuyu, a ghost of loneliness and love, who showed up much earlier, in 1666. She can travel, too.

Finally, there's Okiku, ghost of a peasant girl. She has existed for hundreds of years, too. She lives in wells.

A long time ago, Okiku, a poor, lovely peasant girl worked as a servant in Himeji Castle. Her beauty captured the interest of a samurai knight who served the lord of the castle. His name was Aoyama, and he wanted the humble girl to love him. But Okiku didn't have feelings for Aoyama, and time after time, she turned him down. He schemed to change her mind.

It was Okiku's job to care for a precious set of ten china plates, the prized possession of the lord of Himeji Castle. Aoyama secretly broke one of these, and ten precious plates became nine. He then laid the blame on Okiku, telling her that only he could save her from the great lord's wrath.

Still Okiku refused to have anything to do with the cruel Aoyama. In a rage Aoyama pulled his long sword from its sheath and killed Okiku. He threw her body down the castle well.

But Okiku was to have the last word. Her spirit stayed in the well, forever its resident. And in the dark of every night, at the Hour of the Ox, Okiku's ghost rises from that well. She counts her precious china plates: One, two, three, four . . . and up to nine. But she cannot count that tenth plate, because it's missing. Instead, she screams a scream no living being can forget. It's said if you hear that scream, you may die!

Oiwa is a ghost who chases after her husband, Iemon, who cast her aside in favor of a younger, richer wife. Oiwa traces back to a woman who died in 1636, and the shrine now survives in a Tokyo neighborhood. Oiwa's hate and anger are legendary, and she appears everywhere in Japanese literature and film. You do NOT want to cross her!

The luckless Okiku has lived in wells ever since she broke—of all things—a dinner plate.

Otsuyu is a ghost of a different kind. She worked her way into the heart of an unsuspecting widower named Ogiwara Shinnojō (OH-GEE-WAH-RAH SHIN-NO-JO). An elderly neighbor happened to see the happy couple as they met in Ogiwara's house and warned Ogiwara that his lover was a ghost. Ogiwara parted company with Otsuyu, but he missed her so deeply, he went in search of her—and disappeared. Only later, when Otsuyu's coffin was inspected, did Ogiwara's body show up—there in the coffin with Otsuyu's bones.

One more thing about Oiwa, Otsuyu, and Okiku: They have major hair. Lots of long, flowing, scary hair that artists have drawn for three hundred years. Okay, you might say, ghosts in the West have big hair as well. But in Japan, historically a woman's hair is carefully coiffed, always worn up on the head and always under control. In the prints and paintings of Japanese *yūrei*, however, female ghosts' hair is—hair-raising. In life, no proper woman would have been seen in public with locks like these.

Many, if not most, Japanese honor their ancestors in a special way. The Japanese keep detailed family histories and take good care of family graves. The dead watch over the living, and the living watch over the dead.

Each region across the country celebrates *Obon*, the yearly holiday when the Japanese welcome the spirits of the dead, who return to visit the living. The dead are said to visit during the seventh lunar month. In the old days, lanterns lit the night for the spirits to find their way home. Offerings of food are placed in shrines in family homes and temples. Often families travel to their hometowns.

In Kyoto, Japan's revered holy city, bonfires blaze on hillsides as the celebration *Obon* closes to ensure the dead find their way back to their own land. Many people also float lanterns on streams and lakes to lead the dead back to where they belong.

Oiwa, a ghost of hate, has shown up across Japan for two hundred years.

CHAPTER TWELVE

HARROWING CAROLING WITH HOLIDAY HAUNTS

EACH YEAR BEFORE HALLOWEEN AND CHRISTMAS, THE *oldest bookstore in the world* hosts ghost tours. That would be at the Moravian Book Shop in Bethlehem, Pennsylvania, which opened for business in 1745. Sure, you might say, it makes sense to take a ghost tour in October. But December? And why a bookstore?

The locals say that Bethlehem is filled with ghosts, and that Christmastime is perfect for taking ghost walks by candlelight. Bethlehem, in fact, has claimed the title of "Christmas City" since 1937. Visitors flock into town to take cheer.

Europeans first came to Bethlehem in 1735, when a group of Moravian immigrants arrived from their homes in Germany. The Moravians are among history's oldest Protestants; their roots are in 1500s Czechoslovakia. Like many European arrivals to the American colonies in the 1700s, they hoped to worship freely.

When the Moravians first settled Bethlehem and nearby Nazareth, Pennsylvania, the faithful would walk from Nazareth to Bethlehem on Christmas Eve. The sound of hymn singing rang out on that road. That tradition has died out, but it's still a memory that people cherish.

"Of course, the processions have long since faded away as transportation got better and more churches were built in their home communities," said Kristy Houston, who worked at the Moravian Book Shop. "But it does seem that the processions have not quite faded away *entirely*. Many people who live on the old roads that connect Nazareth and Bethlehem say that on Christmas Eve they will hear this large choir of singers coming down the road, and they go outside expecting to find Christmas carolers, and no one is there."

Bethlehem is home to God's Acre Cemetery, a stop on the ghost tour. Ghost hunters have carried sound equipment with them to record their tours, with some chilly results.

"They were recording it, and when they listened back to their tapes, they heard something more than just their tour,"

Houston said. "Very clearly, speaking over their guide's voice, they heard another voice that no one heard at the time, [and] nobody recognized. The message it left was very simple and clear: 'Leave please.'"

Apparently the cemetery's residents wanted to rest in peace.

DAY OF THE DEAD, DÍA DE LOS MUERTOS

Days draw short. The harvest is in. Monarch butterflies are returning to their cold-weather home. Winter is coming, but first, there are ancestors to remember!

As the calendar flips from October to November, families of Latino or Hispanic heritage celebrate a festival with roots so deep, they tangle with ancient holidays.

The first two days of November mark the Day of the Dead, Día de los Muertos (DEE-uh day los MWER-tos).

This child helps his family celebrate Día de Muertos (Day of the Dead) at a tomb decorated with marigolds and candles near Mexico City in 2019.

'Tis the season across Mexico, Central America, and the American Southwest when families gather in cemeteries to clean the graves of their departed. After all, the spirits of their beloved relatives and friends will soon arrive from the afterlife to join the festivities.

Take note: Don't confuse Halloween with Day of the Dead. These are not the same.

Those who wait by the graves set out bright yellow marigolds to catch the eye of these spirits and direct them homeward. Picnics and parties with music and dance take place in cemeteries. In cities and towns, people celebrate with parades and parties, as well. They feast on special home-cooked foods (many families have their own tamal recipes) and pan de Muertos—oval-shaped bread of the dead.

At home, families create *ofrendas* (o-FREN-das), shrines in memory of their departed relatives, with photos, flowers, foods, and sugar skulls decorated with brightly colored icing. Decorations, paintings, and sculptures of skulls and skeletons play a huge part in the festival.

These *calaveras* (kah-lah-VER-as) and *calacas* (kah-LAH-kas), skulls and bones, reach back to very old traditions of the Aztecs and others who lived in Mexico before the Spanish arrived. The Aztecs understood death as a mark of the never-ending cycle of human experience: birth, life, and death. As with other indigenous beliefs, the ways

Aztecs honored their dead melded with Roman Catholic feast days—in this case, All Saints and All Souls Days on November 1 and 2. The Catholic feast days are rather solemn. By contrast, Day of the Dead is a time of joy.

Author's Note: Just as I was finishing this book, I stopped into a small neighborhood grocery on a trip to Chicago. It was late October. As I was chatting with the manager about all the skulls I saw in the store, I mentioned Day of the Dead. He told me that for many years on the holiday, when he was a boy, his mother set out a picture of his deceased father. Along with the picture, his mother placed a breakfast dish, something his father had liked, which sat out for about half an hour before they shared it.

I asked him how old he was when his father died. "Five," he replied.

As so many other immigrants have done, and still do, his mom had brought with her family traditions to help start a new life. From Mexico to Chicago, his family had not forgotten Día de Los Muertos.

SUSSING THE SOUNDS AT SANDRINGHAM

Great Britain's royal family has its share of ghosting, according to what newspapers say. Reportedly weird stuff begins to happen close to Christmas.

Most of the great palaces in England don't belong to Queen Elizabeth II, but Her Majesty does in fact own a big country estate in Sandringham northwest of London. Every year the royal family gathers to spend Christmas there. It's a big crowd, and reportedly a crew of ghosts is there to greet them. Staff at Sandringham have told newspapers over the years that weird presences follow them around, and Christmas cards fly out of walls.

It wasn't always that way. The *Illustrated London News*, a most respectable newspaper that was read across the empire, had this to say about the grand home in 1887. Edward, Prince of Wales, and family had lived in their country retreat for a while. There was no talk of ghosts.

Sandringham is the haunted estate where the British royal family often spends their Christmas.

> For the house itself, it is so completely and simply a
> country gentleman's house that it seems an impertinence
> to describe it. There are no "show-rooms" for the public,
> and as it has been in existence but 15 years, no traditions
> have had time to gather round it: nor could any man be
> so unreasonable as to expect a ghost.

A ghost? Presumably the house had to hang around longer than fifteen years in order to build some history.

Do you remember Prince Albert Victor, who sailed aboard HMS *Bacchante* and saw the *Flying Dutchman* off the coast of South Africa? The one who died too young in 1892?

He died at Sandringham.

When Kate Middleton married Prince William in 2012, a web version of one of England's tell-all tabloids speculated that the new princess would celebrate "a haunted first Christmas at Sandringham." Apparently the house has now been around long enough to pick up a few ghosts.

> [I]n the mid-1980s, Prince Charles was looking for some
> old prints with his valet Ken Stronach when they both
> suddenly felt very cold. They were convinced someone
> was behind them . . . but no one was there.
>
> Our shadowy source [whoever spoke to the *Mirror's*
> reporter] said: "After crying, 'Oh heck!' the Prince

grabbed the first print and got out as quickly as he could. He was petrified.

"There have been lots of incidents in the library. There is an old clock in there and the hands move by themselves. There is a smaller part of the library where a servant once had a kip [nap], only to be woken by books flying from the shelves."

In 1996, footman Shaun Croasdale fled the cellar screaming after believing he saw the ghost of the Queen's favourite servant, Tony Jarred, who had died a year earlier. The Queen invited Shaun to share his experience.

"She believed every word. There was never any question of him being sacked for going potty!"

That's Britspeak for going batty. Or off his rocker. You get the picture.

CHRISTMAS TREES LOST AT SEA

By the late 1800s, many American families who celebrated Christmas had taken to the German tradition of decorating trees for Christmas. These were cut fresh in the woods.

In Chicago, Illinois, Christmas trees began to arrive by boat. The *Rouse Simmons*, a wooden schooner powered by wind, typically carried lumber from northern Michigan to Chicago, about a five-day voyage. But in late November, its cargo switched to spruce trees, delivered fresh to a dock where the Chicago River met Lake Michigan.

At the ship's helm was Captain Herman Schuenemann. Purportedly he was a kindhearted man, and many of the trees he carried were meant for orphanages or homes of the poor.

When Schuenemann grew older and stepped back from work, another captain, Charles Nelson, took charge. But at Christmastime in 1912, Schuenemann decided to make the trip as well. A week before Thanksgiving, the *Rouse Simmons* left Manistique Harbor in northern Michigan, bound for

Captain William Schuenemann (center) went down with the Christmas Tree Ship during a November gale.

Chicago. On board were seventeen sailors and five thousand Christmas trees.

A gale blew up across Lake Michigan's ice-cold waters. There was no kind of radio communication between ship and shore. Two days later, observers at the U.S. Lifesaving Service station in Sturgeon Bay, Wisconsin, saw the *Simmons* "on the horizon with sails tattered, hull encased in ice, riding low in the water and flying distress signals." They telephoned the Two Rivers station twenty miles to the south, which launched a Coast Guard powerboat to the rescue. But there was no sign of the *Rouse Simmons*.

The "Christmas Tree Ship" had gone down, leaving no trace of trees or the seventeen souls on board.

In a brave move, Schuenemann's widow, Barbara, held fast to her family Christmas tradition. Trees continued to come by ship, then by rail, every year until she died in 1933.

Signs of the sunken ship floated to Lake Michigan's surface or washed ashore. At first it was trees, entangled in fishermen's nets. Then there was a note in a bottle, signed by Captain Nelson, saying the ship was in distress. Not until 1971 did a diver named Gordon Kent Bellrichard find the *Rouse Simmons*, one hundred and eighty feet (fifty-five meters) below the surface of Lake Michigan. She was six miles from shore.

As the *Grand Haven Tribune* reported in 2015, the *Rouse Simmons* sails on as a full-blown ghost story.

After her sinking, especially on Christmas Eve and Christmas Day, sailors have reported seeing a ghost ship with glistening, ice-covered Christmas trees on its deck. Also, it is claimed sailors hear human cries in the wind and bells ringing as if sounding an alarm of an impending storm. Some eyewitnesses of the ghost ship have claimed to see a person waving a lighted lantern back and forth on deck.

Put these chilling words into your mind's eye. How's that for a cold and creepy Christmas story?

"All you could see was trees," said Rich Evenhouse after a dive to the *Rouse Simmons* shipwreck in Lake Michigan.

The Brown Lady of Raynham Hall is among England's most revered ghosts. She has hung around since 1726. Here she is photographed by *Country Life* magazine in 1936.

AFTERWORD

TWO MORE STORIES NOT FAR FROM HOME

NOW THAT YOU'VE READ UP ON SOME OF THE thousands of ghosts out there, I'd like to tell you two more tales. As with my sister, Anne's, story, I didn't have to go very far from home to find them.

This time, it was my nephew, Tom Hollihan, who informed me that he'd seen a ghost of a small boy many times. I was quite surprised!

A bit of background: After high school, Tommy (as I know him) moved in with a family in Natrona, Pennsylvania. "Natrona" refers to natron—salt—that was mined and processed along the Allegheny River, twenty-five miles east of Pittsburgh. In the mid-1800s a town grew up around that area, and the Penn Salt Company built houses for its workers. Some were large, for the men who ran the company, while the midlevel employee homes were smaller and built close together. Lower-level workers lived in brick row houses that shared side walls. Tom lived in one of these. He calls Natrona a steel town, but it was more a salt- and coal-mining town (Names of its residents have been changed for reasons of privacy):

The back of the house where Tommy Hollihan saw Kevin Homeburger.

When I graduated high school [in 2012], my friend Megan and I, her two brothers, Ethan (8) and Kevin (4), her father and mother and "our" Grampa, moved out of an old coal-mining house . . . and bought a row house in the hundred-year-old steel town of Natrona. We purchased it from the mother of one of Megan's father's friends, who we will call Stumpy. Stumpy had lived in the house for five years and then left it vacant for eight years until we bought it. The basement door, which had glass windowpanes, was in the living room in the center of the first floor. Stumpy would swear on his life that he could see the face of a child peeking at him through that door when he was sitting on his couch. It had him so spooked he would refuse to enter the basement, even when a fuse had blown or the pilot light [on the furnace] had gone out. He'd call someone else to come do it. He was that convinced.

A while after these "occurrences" began, he heard from a local, a Natrona native, that during the construction of this particular row of row houses, which were built in the 1890s, a young boy had been killed while playing amongst the foundations and heavy equipment on our street . . .

But anyhoo, Stumpy is not the main character of this tale. Fast-forward a decade, we buy the house, we move in, we start cleaning the place up, and Kevin, who is four, suddenly has an imaginary friend, who he's affectionately named Kevin Homeburger. Kevin Homeburger, according to Kevin, was living in our house when we moved in, and he has very old shoes. So we go about our life with the imaginary Kevin Homeburger, and all is regular, except for, let's say . . . a few odd events.

. . . I'm in the kitchen, and the kids have their little friends over, and I feel a tug on the back of my shirt, and I turn around to see what I'm needed for, simply to find that there's no one behind me, or even in the same room with me. Or . . . I'm getting ready for work, sitting on the couch, drinking my coffee, listening to the kids play upstairs in their room, only to eventually remember that the kids are in fact at school, and I'm alone in the house. Little occurrences, just like that.

And then, about two months into living in this house, I land a full-time utility position . . . I come home at the same time every night—I walk in my front door at 9:30, into the front room that Grampa and I share as a bedroom, and plop down on my couch, exhausted, and with aching feet. Every night. It's my ritual. Come in, take a load off, and chat with Grampa for an hour or so before even getting up to take off my boots.

Well, I'll tell ya, every night sitting on that couch I'd see the same thing. On the landing at the top of the staircase, which was the only thing separating our front room from the living room with the ghastly basement door, I would see, out of the corner of my eye, a child playing. I'd be talking to Grampa, making eye contact with him on his bed across the room from my couch, and up on that landing to my left was this child.

And I'd turn to yell at Kevin, thinking he was up past his bedtime and out of his room, and lo and behold, as soon as I'd look directly at the landing, there'd be nothing there. I must have imagined it! I go back to my conversation with Grampa, and not twenty or thirty seconds later, there that child would be again, clear as day out of the corner of my eye, playing on that landing. Out of habit, I turn to yell at Kevin again, and—nothing!

Not a soul in sight, save for Grampa and myself.

This went on EVERY NIGHT. I'd mention it casually, we'd laugh and tell Kevin Homeburger to go to bed with the kids, and we let it become a part of our daily routine. Every night. It never ceased to be.

After a few more months, I moved out . . . but Grampa, the kids, and their mom and dad all remained in that house. A few years later, Grampa moved out and got a house down the street, and when I'd go to visit him, we'd sometimes talk about ol' Kevin Homeburger. Until the day Grampa died, he maintained that there was definitely "one extra kid" there, even if no one saw him. Even as Kevin grew, and lost interest in Kevin Homeburger, to this day, whenever Stumpy [comes back to] that house, he makes no eye contact with that basement door, claiming to us that the face of that child will sometimes be there, looking back at him. After all these years.

. . . And after all these years, here we have an up-to-date ghost story, so much like many older ones you've read on these pages!

∿

You may ask: Do I believe in ghosts?

Only once in my life did I ever see anything paranormal. In the mid-1990s, I took our big black Lab, Maverick, on a walk around the block in my home city of Blue Ash, Ohio. It's not the usual city block, but more a set of winding streets built on farmland first owned by a man named Solomon Ferris back in the early 1800s. There's a mix of homes: some built in the 1950s and newer ones in the 1990s. At one end of the neighborhood is the brick Solomon Ferris House, built in 1826. About a quarter mile east is a wooden farmhouse he built for his son, Solomon Ferris Jr., and his new bride, Mary. It was finished in 1864.

Maverick and I were out at dusk. I decided to take a short cut home by walking down a quiet road and cutting through my neighbors' yards. I was heading toward Solomon Jr.'s house as it was getting dark. It was then that I noticed two small white figures scurry down the left side of the road and run up a tree trunk. I didn't say anything about it at the time, but in my mind's eye I still can picture the event.

Years went by, and eventually some of my neighbors "downsized" and moved to other parts of Blue Ash. We still get together, and, in the summer of 2018, one former neighbor had a bunch of us to her new place for a picnic. A few of us sat on her deck sharing news about our kids, now adults, and other chatter. I was talking about writing a book about ghosts and mentioned—for the very first time—that I'd seen these two small ghosts climbing a tree back when I was walking my dog twenty-plus years ago.

After I finished my story, another former neighbor named Pam came outside to join us. Pam and her family had lived in a house to the west of Solomon Jr.'s place. Their yards touched.

Okay, I thought, here's a chance to tell my story to someone else. So I brought up the topic again and asked Pam if she'd ever seen a ghost in the neighborhood.

"Yes," Pam said. She had seen ghosts, once, as she looked out her window and across her yard. One evening, she'd seen two small figures, holding hands, running toward the old farmhouse that Solomon Ferris had built for his son.

I just about fell out of my chair. Pam had corroborated what I'd seen at the same location. I'd been walking south, and she'd been looking from a different location, but both of us had spotted the same pair of little ghosts—"looking like they were holding hands," Pam said. "One was bigger than the other."

There's a good history book about Blue Ash that talks about the Ferris family. If you look at the record, two children born to Solomon Jr. and Mary Ferris didn't reach adulthood. One was as an infant boy named Stanley, and the other, a little girl named Martha, died when she was six or seven.

Two small children. Two little ghosts.

It's all left me shaking my head in wonder . . .

NOTES

INTRODUCTION

vi "No": Tia F. with the author, August 2018.

vi "Maybeeeeee": Carlie R., ibid.

vi "But there's a girl in our class, and she talks to them all the time!": Tia F. and Carlie R., ibid.

x "boggles, Bloody Bones, spirits, demons ...": Michael Aislabie Denham and James Hardy, ed. *The Denham Tracts: A Collection of Folklore*, reprinted from the Original Tracts and Pamphlets Printed by Denham Between 1846 and 1859, vol. 2 (London: Folklore Society, 1895), 76–80.

CHAPTER ONE: THE DEATHLY DOMESTICATED—GHOST DOGS AND CATS

3 "I had been on my knees pounding away ...": W. H. C. Pynchon, "The Black Dog," *Connecticut Quarterly*, vol. 4, 1898, 155, archive.org/details /connecticutquart02hart/page/153.

4 "Then we turned back and started for home ...": Ibid., 156.

4 "The dog still trotted on ahead ...": Ibid., 157.

5 "We talked till late that night ...": Ibid., 158.

5 "The mass of broken fragments of rock ... then the fun began ...": Ibid., 159.

5 [B]y scrambling, crawling and wriggling ...": Ibid.

6 "So long as we were in the sunlight ...": Ibid., 159–160.

6 "I did not believe it before ...": Ibid., 160.

7 "brought back the body of poor Marshall": Ibid.

8 "If you read about old buildings ...": Steve Livengood, author interview, June 16, 2018.

9 "The Capitol in Washington is probably the most thoroughly haunted building in the world ... The Demon Cat is said to have made its appearance again": *Butte Weekly Miner*, Sunday, October 4, 1898, 4. See www. newspapers.com/search/#lnd=1&query=The+Demon +Cat+is+said+to+have+made+its+appearance+again%2C+after+many +years+ of+absence.&t=7951.

10 "One of the oldest stories is recounted by newsman John Alexander ...": "Capitol Police," *Congressional Record: Proceedings and Debates of the U.S.*

Congress, vol. 127(2) (Washington, D.C.: Govt. Print. Off., February 1981), 1535.

15 "I was cleaning up during the day and walked upstairs …": Melinda Sedelmeyer, author interview, June 18, 2018.

CHAPTER TWO: GHOSTS GO TO SCHOOL

16 "Anyone have the number for ghostbusters?": "Coláiste Éamann Rís— Cork City," Facebook.com post, October 2017.

17 "we've been very busy … crazy with the ghost …": Aaron Wolfe, author interview, September 17, 2018.

18 "At four a.m. … they heard all kinds of noises going off": Ibid.

18 "toilet door that locked itself from the inside … Our boys don't use it anymore": Ibid.

19 "At five a.m. the man clearly heard the sound of a trumpet …": Ibid.

19 "I swear, it was insane": Ibid.

23 "Quite how bad the man's regime …": Rupert Matthews, *Haunted York* (Stroud, Gloucestershire: History Press, 2014), 52.

23 "When a child died, the church …": Lisa Crawford. "Haunted York," BBC, York and North Yorkshire: Local History, November 13, 2014, www.bbc.co.uk/northyorkshire/content/articles/2008/10/29 /haunted_york_feature.

24 "Several of those working on the site …": Matthews, "Haunted York," 52.

25 "everyone in the village was aware … 'don't want to send our children to school.'": Indranil Sarkar, "It's a Holiday, Thank the Ghosts," *Telegraph* (Kolkata, West Bengal, India), July 15, 2007, www.telegraphindia .com/1070716/asp/bengal/story_8064496.asp.

CHAPTER THREE: WEIRD WRAITHS IN WHITE SPACES

26 "Just two months ago today …": *Harry S. Truman Papers*, Harry S. Truman Library, www.trumanlibrary.gov/library/truman-papers /correspondence-harry-s-truman-bess-wallace-truman-1921–1959 /june-12-1945.

28 "I slept well but hot …": Ibid; www.trumanlibrary.gov/library/ truman-papers/correspondence-harry-s-truman-bess-wallace-truman -1921–1959/september-9-1946.

28 "People all over the country are asking …": Robert Klara, *The Hidden White House: Harry Truman and the Reconstruction of America's Most Famous Residence.* (New York: St. Martin's Press, 2013) 75.

29   "It seems that the White House is haunted …": William Bushong, "Forgotten Ghosts of the White House," White House Historical Association, www.whitehousehistory.org/the-forgotten-ghosts-that -haunted-the-white-house.

30   "a towering rage … he thinks it will be a very serious thing": Ibid.

30   "White House Is Notorious Haunt of Ghosts": *Washington Herald*, March 2, 1913, chroniclingamerica.loc.gov/lccn/sn83045433 /1913-03-02/ed-1/seq-29.

31   "is always seen walking up the stairs …": Ibid.

33   "The hair on the back of our neck …": Ted Johnson, "Is the White House Haunted? Jenna and Barbara Bush Share Their Ghost Story," *Variety*, October 31, 2017, variety.com/2017/politics/news/bush-sisters-white -house-ghosts-1202603176.

34   "I do a lot of evening programs …": Steve Livengood, interview with the author, June 11, 2018.

35   "He objected to giving medals …": Ibid.

35   "Ghost of Anne Boleyn at the Tower": *New York Times*, September 18, 1897, timesmachine.nytimes.com/timesmachine/1897/09/19 /102062282.pdf.

38   "Well, an old friend of mine, Captain …": "Anne Boleyn's Ghost at the Tower," *The Psychological Review: A Cosmopolitan Organ of Spiritualism and Psychological Research*, vol. 4 (January to June 1882); 220–221, books.google.com/books?id=d_APAAAAYAAJ&pg=PA220&dq=anne +boleyn+ghost&hl=en&sa=X&ved=0ahUKEwiP28_2uLHdAhWG2lM KHV2gDlUQ6AEIYTAK#v=onepage&q=anne%20boleyn%20 ghost&f=false.

CHAPTER FOUR: GHOSTLY HITCHHIKERS, BANDITS, AND A LADY IN WHITE

41   "These two boys were driving down a country road …": Jane Albright and Delana Good, collector, "Vanishing Hitchhiker," Vigo County Historical Society, Vigo County, Indiana, reprinted with permission, visions.indstate.edu:8888/cdm/singleitem/collection/folklore/id/2794/ rec/1.

41   "nice and lovely girl" and "a prophecy of wars and plagues": Bennett, Gillian. "The Vanishing Hitchhiker at Fifty-Five." *Western Folklore*. Winter 1998, 57, l; ProQuest Central. p. 7.

42 "the merest tyro …": Mrs. James Sadler, "The Story of Lady Maud," *Our Young People. Published for the Benefit of the Deaf-Mutes, at St. Francis, Wis.* (November 1911), 144.

42 "I was driving the 8:30 train to the North …": Doris Jones-Baker, *The Folklore of Hertfordshire* (Totowa, New Jersey: Rowman and Littlefield 1977), 89–90.

43 "It was just when we were passing through … in my life": Ibid, 89–90.

44 "I soon noticed … the train was slowing": Ibid, 89–90.

44 "the home signal stood for line clear … stop that express …": Ibid, 89–90.

44 "Heaven alone knows …": Ibid. p. 89–90.

45 "Young Ali went to study for his BA in the United States …": John William Johnson, "The Vanishing Hitchhiker in Africa," *Research in African Literatures*, vol. 38, no. 3, *The Preservation and Survival of African Oral Literature* (Fall 2007): 24–33. Reprinted with permission from the Indiana University Press.

47 "My friends and I decided to find out for ourselves what is true and what is not …": "Clinton Road: A Dark Ride," Weird N.J., weirdnj.com /stories/clinton-road.

52 "She supposedly drowned her daughter or son …": Antonia Quintana Pigno, "Along the Creek Behind St. Catherine's: Hispanic Folklore of Emporia, Kansas," *Kansas Quarterly*, vol. 25, no. 2, 1993, 87–95.

52 "Well, where we used to live …": Ibid.

53 "La Llorona is a fixture in the Mexican and Mexican American communities…" Ibid.

53 "I can't stress how important she is to our culture": Antonia Quintana Pigno, email to the author, September 11, 2018.

54 "Really confusing … Was he a criminal or was he out to protect his family?": Craig Powell, interview with the author, May 9, 2019.

56 "We put ourselves in situations …": Ibid.

56 "Vibing …": Ibid.

56 "It was as if Ned Kelly was sitting there …": Ibid.

57 "When we immerse ourselves … Is that you, Ned?": Ibid.

58 "I'm reading and researching and learning": Ibid.

59 "A stagehand offered to take them down …": Scott Santangelo, interview with the author, November 14, 2018.

60 "My parents were healers …": "About the Author," Ghostbooks.biz, www.ghostbooks.biz/about-author.html.

62 "Then from out of the bushes ...": Antonio R. Garcez, *American Indian Ghost Stories of the West* (Moriarty, New Mexico: Red Rabbit Press, 2017), 61.

62 "The man stopped ...": Ibid., 61–62.

63 "As he re-entered the brush ...": Ibid., 62.

64 Antonio Garcez, email to the author, July 13, 2018.

CHAPTER FIVE: A TREASURE TROVE OF GHOSTLY GUARDIANS

68 "Like so many places—possible and impossible ...": J. H. Temple and George Sheldon, *A History of the Town of Northfield, Massachusetts, for 150 years, With an Account of the Territory by the Squakheags; and with Family Genealogies,* (Albany: Joel Munsell, 1875), 18. See archive.org/stream/historyoftownofn00temp#page/18/mode/1up/search/kidd.

71 "The writer found two ex-slaves sitting on the porch ...": "FOLK-LORE: EX-SLAVES," *Federal Writers' Project: Slave Narrative Project, vol. 14, South Carolina, Part 2, Eddington-Hunter* (1936), 97–99. Manuscript/Mixed Material. www.loc.gov/item/mesn142.

71 "She had seen ghosts two or three times": Ibid.

CHAPTER SIX: FLYERS, FOLLIES, WHISTLERS, DOLLIES, AND A MEDIUM

75 "That's not funny,": John G. Fuller, *The Ghost of Flight 401* (New York: G. P. Putnam's Sons, 1976), xi.

75 "Carl Sandburg once said ...": Ibid., xiii.

77 "became almost intolerable": Ibid., 159.

77 "immediately hit with a cold, very clammy feeling ...": Ibid., 159.

78 "Out of the corner of her [Ginny's] eye": Ibid., 159.

80 "I beg your pardon, Captain": Ibid., 167.

80 "Then he froze": Ibid., 167.

81 "double take": Ibid., 192.

81 "Watch out for fire on this airplane": Ibid., 192.

86 "We sat again for materialization": Peter Aykroyd, *A History of Ghosts: The True Story of Séances, Mediums, Ghosts, and Ghostbusters* (New York: Rodale, 2009), 28.

CHAPTER SEVEN: GHOSTS MAKE WAR

90 "Toward the center of Lee's line Confederate troops positioned themselves …": Brandon Marie Miller, *Robert E. Lee: The Man, the Soldier, the Myth* (New York: Kane/Calkins Creek, 2019), 144.

92 "'It was as if it grabbed me by the leg …' 'It got to me so much …'": Michael E. Ruane, "Ghosts of the Union's Black Soldiers Rise from Loudoun County's Past," *Washington Post*, March 2, 2013, www.washingtonpost.com/local/ghosts-of-the-unions-black-soldiers -rise-from-loudoun-countys-past/2013/03/02/2273e41e-7f7c-11e2 -8074-b26a871b165a_story.html?utm_term=.ed3d04bac9e9.

97 "It is in this phase of the battle …": Michael Fassbender, "The Legend of the Angel of Mons," *Depth and Integration*, michaeltfassbender. com/nonfiction/the-world-wars/miscellaneous/the-legend-of-the -angel-of-mons.

97 "Then there is the story of the 'Angel of Mons' …": Peter Clowes, "Angels and Archers at Mons," *Military History*, August 1, 2001, vol. 18, no. 3, 65.

97 "Then came the torrid [hot] days of Mons": Hereward Carrington, *Psychical Phenomena and the War* (New York: American Universities Publishing Co., 1920), 345.

98 "There was an F. R. A. man …": Ibid., 347–348.

100 "I hesitate to tell the story": Sydney A. Moseley, *The Truth About the Dardanelles* (London: Cassell and Company, Ltd., 1916), 70–73.

CHAPTER EIGHT: GHOSTS RIDE THE RAILS

106 "Waiting for the Train": Adam Selzer, "Lincoln's Phantom Funeral Train Described in 1872," *Mysterious Chicago*, February 22, 2014, mysteriouschicago.com/lincolns-phantom-funeral- train -described-in-1872.

109 "We sat there for about an hour …": Dave Yanko, "The St. Louis Ghost Train," *Virtual Saskatchewan*, [no date] www.virtualsk.com/current _issue/ghost_train.html.

110 "We drove and drove and drove … And all of a sudden the light was gone …": Ibid.

110 "The place was wild in this light, kind of forlorn": Phil Campagna, "The St. Louis Ghost Train Light . . . Explained!", www.philcampagna.com /stlouisghostlight/ghost.html.

110 "They must have noticed . . . others fast behind": Ibid.

111 "The thought of catching that ghost on camera . . .": Ibid.

111 "They pulled up, and I rolled down my window . . .": Ibid.

113 "Railroad Bill . . . alongside the track" and "People would hide him— until he shot the sheriff": Don Sales, author interview, November 19, 2019.

113 "So the sheriff decided Railroad Bill must be hiding under the low bushes . . .": Ben Berntson, "Railroad Bill," *Encyclopedia of Alabama*, www.encyclopediaofalabama.org/article/h-1258.

114 "All the people believed that he was magical and mystical . . .": Don Sales, author interview, November 19, 2019.

114 "One Negro woman made a great speech . . .": Burgin Mathews, "Looking for Railroad Bill," *Southern Cultures*, vol. 9, no. 3 (Fall 2003), 83.

116 "[I]t is only seen after midnight . . .": Eric Grundhauser, "The Silver Arrow, the Real Ghost Train Haunting the Stockholm Metro," *Atlas Obscura*, October 7, 2015, www.atlasobscura.com/articles/ the-silver-arrow-the-real-ghost-train-haunting-the-stockholm-metro.

116 "I would say the legend about Silverpilen is very much alive today . . .": Johanna Bergström, email to the author, August 2, 2018.

117 "The story when I was growing up in the 1990s . . .": Ibid.

CHAPTER NINE: HAUNTS IN RED SPACES

129 "She felt her arms clenched in a strong masculine grip . . .": Alan Murdie, "The Ghost of Oliver Cromwell (1599–1658)," *EuroParanormal*, europaranormal.com/ghosts/the-ghost-of-oliver-cromwell-1599-1658.

130 "His daughter, Abigail, had been away . . .": "England's Most Famous Ghost at Painswick & Chavenage," Cotswolds.info, www.cotswolds. info/strange-things/englands-most-famous-ghost.shtml.

131 "Cromwell's head passed into the hands of the Wilkinson family . . .": Nicholas Rogers, email to the author, December 11, 2019.

134 "being held up by termites holding hands": Paul Biasco, "Chicago British Pub Red Lion Prepares to Reopen in Lincoln Park," DNA Info, April 14, 2014, www.dnainfo.com/chicago/20140414/lincoln-park /chicago-british-pub-red-lion-prepares-reopen-lincoln-park.

135 "I would see a light settle on people …": Dubnick and Weagly, *Tales*, vi.

135 "The photo in the room they shared …": John Garwell, email to the author, December 3, 2019.

CHAPTER TEN: GHOSTS SET SAIL

139 "1881. WE MEET THE *FLYING DUTCHMAN* …": Albert Victor, Duke of Clarence and Avondale, and Prince George of Wales, *The Cruise of Her Majesty's Ship "BACCHANTE" 1879–1882* (London: Macmillan and Co., 1886), 551, www.google.com/books/edition/The_Cruise_of _Her _Majesty_s_Ship_Bacchan/LL7o7AF-DIwC?hl=en&gbpv=0.

140 "At 6.15 A.M. observed land (Mount Diana) to the north-east …": Ibid., 551.

142 "Over and over, people on both sides of the strait …": "Hair-Raising Canadian Ghost Stories!", *Canada Post*, June 13, 2014. See www. canadapost.ca/web/en/blogs/consumer/details.page?article=2014/06 /13/5_haunted_canada_sta&cattype=Consumer&cat=mailandmore.

142 "Hundreds of shipwrecks … seafarers": Ibid.

143 "It was bright white and gold and looked like a schooner with three masts …": "Phantom Ship Spotted by Visitor," *Truro News*, www. trurodaily.com/lifestyles/phantom-ship-spotted-by-visitor-151203.

CHAPTER ELEVEN: HOT SUMMERS, CHILLING GHOSTS

150 "when souls go to the afterlife … angry ghosts": Ran Lee, author interview, July 4, 2018.

151 "*Yūrei* … follow certain rules, obey …": Zack Davisson, *Yūrei: The Japanese Ghost* (Seattle: Chin Music Press, 2015), 22.

152 "slowly dragged up to a giant sucking black hole in the ceiling …": Ibid., 20.

CHAPTER TWELVE: HARROWING CAROLING WITH HOLIDAY HAUNTS

158 "Of course, the processions have long since faded away … But it does seem that …": Margie Peterson, "'Tis the season for ghost stories in Bethlehem," *The Morning Call*, December 16, 2015. See www.mcall.com /entertainment/arts-theater/mc-bethlehem-ghosts-christmas-historic -haunts-20151216-story.html.

158 "They were recording it, and when they listened back …": Ibid.

161 "Five," he replied: William Rendon, author interview, October 26, 2019.

163 "For the house itself, it is so completely …": "English Homes. no. VIII. Sandringham," *Illustrated London News*, vol. XC (January to June 1887), 26, books.google.com/books?id=z-9GAQAAMAAJ&pg=PA26&dq= sandringham+ghost&hl=en&sa=X&ved=0ahUKEwiUz5HD5qbeAh UsrYMKHdH0Ca4Q6AEISzAG#v=onepage&q=sandringham%20 ghost&f=true.

163 "[I]n the mid-1980s, Prince Charles … going potty!'": Susie Boniface, "Kate Middleton Due to Spend a Haunted First Christmas at Sandringham," *Mirror*, December 18, 2011, updated March 15, 2012. See www.mirror.co.uk/news/uk-news/kate-middleton-due-to-spend-a -haunted-97375.

166 "on the horizon … distress signals": Kevin Collier, *Grand Haven Tribune*, July 22, 2015.

167 "After her sinking, especially on Christmas Eve and Christmas Day …": Ibid.

167 "All you could see was trees": Rich Evenhouse, author interview, November 18, 2019.

AFTERWORD

170 "When I graduated high school [in 2012], my friend Morgan and I …": Tom Hollihan, email to the author, May 25, 2018.

175 "Yes … looking like they were holding hands": Pamela Senefeld, interview with the author, July 2018.

SELECT BIBLIOGRAPHY

INTRODUCTION

Denham, Michael Aislabie and James Hardy, ed. *The Denham Tracts: A Collection of Folklore, Reprinted from the Original Tracts and Pamphlets Printed by Denham Between 1846 and 1859*, vol. 2, 76–80. London: Folklore Society, 1895.

CHAPTER ONE: THE DEATHLY DOMESTICATED–GHOST DOGS AND CATS

"Capitol Police." *Congressional Record: Proceedings and Debates of the U.S. Congress*, vol. 127(2), 1535. Government Printing Office (February 1981).

Pynchon, W. H. C. "The Black Dog," *Connecticut Quarterly*, vol. 4, 1898, archive.org/details/connecticutquart02hart/page/153.

"The Demon Cat is said to have made its appearance again." *The Butte Weekly Miner*, October 4, 1898. See www.newspapers.com/search/#lnd=1&query= The+Demon+Cat+is+said+to+have+made+its+appearance+again%2C+ after+many+years+of+absence.&t=7951.

CHAPTER TWO: GHOSTS GO TO SCHOOL

Crawford, Lisa. "Haunted York." BBC, York & North Yorkshire: Local History, November 13, 2014. See www.bbc.co.uk/northyorkshire/content/ articles/2008/10/29/haunted_york_feature.shtml.

Matthews, Rupert. *Haunted York*. Stroud, Gloucestershire, England: The History Press, 2014. NOOK book.

Sarkar, Indranil. "It's a Holiday, Thank the Ghosts," *Telegraph India*, July 15, 2007. See www.telegraphindia.com/1070716/asp/bengal/story _8064496.asp.

CHAPTER THREE: WEIRD WRAITHS IN WHITE SPACES

"Anne Boleyn's Ghost at the Tower," *The Psychological Review: A Cosmopolitan Organ of Spiritualism and Psychological Research*, vol. 4 (January to June 1882). See books.google.com/books?id=d_APAAAAYAAJ&pg =PA220&dq=anne+boleyn+ghost&hl=en&sa=X&ved=0ahUKEwiP28 _2uLHdAhWG2lMKHV2gDIUQ6AEIYTAK#v=onepage&q =anne%20boleyn%20ghost&f=false.

Bushong, William. "Forgotten Ghosts of the White House," White House Historical Association. See www.whitehousehistory.org/the-forgotten -ghosts-that-haunted-the-white-house.

"Ghost of Anne Boleyn at the Tower," *New York Times*, September 18, 1897, timesmachine.nytimes.com/timesmachine/1897/09/19/102062282.pdf.

Harry S. Truman Papers. Harry S. Truman Presidential Library. See www .trumanlibrary.gov.

Johnson, Ted. "Is the White House Haunted? Jenna and Barbara Bush Share Their Ghost Story," *Variety*, October 31, 2017. See variety.com/2017 /politics/news/bush-sisters-white-house-ghosts-1202603176.

Klara, Robert. *The Hidden White House: Harry Truman and the Reconstruction of America's Most Famous Residence*. New York: St. Martin's Press, 2013.

"White House Is Notorious Haunt of Ghosts," *Washington Herald*, March 2, 1913. See chroniclingamerica.loc.gov/lccn/sn83045433/1913-03-02/ed-1 /seq-29.

CHAPTER FOUR: GHOSTLY HITCHHIKERS, BANDITS, AND A LADY IN WHITE

Albright, Jane and Delana Good, collector. "Vanishing Hitchhiker." Vigo County Historical Society. Vigo County, Indiana. Reprinted with permission from the Vigo County Historical Society. See visions.indstate .edu:8888/cdm/singleitem/collection/folklore/id/2794/rec/1.

Bennett, Gillian. "The Vanishing Hitchhiker at Fifty-Five," *Western Folklore*, vol. 57, no. 1 (Winter 1998): 7.

"Clinton Road: A Dark Ride," Weird N.J., weirdnj.com/stories/clinton-road.

Fuller, Amy. "The Wailing Woman," *History Today*, October 31, 2017. See www.historytoday.com/miscellanies/wailing-woman.

Garcez, Antonio R., *American Indian Ghosts Stories of the West*. New Mexico: Red Rabbit Press, 2017.

Johnson, John William. "The Vanishing Hitchhiker in Africa," *Research in African Literatures*, vol. 38, no. 3. *The Preservation and Survival of African Oral Literature* (Fall 2007): 24–33. Reprinted with permission of Indiana University Press.

Jones-Baker, Doris. *The Folklore of Hertfordshire*. Totowa, New Jersey: Rowman and Littlefield, 1977.

Krauss, Clifford. "After 500 Years, Cortes's Girlfriend Is Not Forgiven," *New York Times*, March 26, 1997. See www.nytimes.com/1997/03/26/world /after-500-years-cortes-s-girlfriend-is-not-forgiven.html.

Pigno, Antonia Quintana. "Along the Creek Behind St. Catherine's: Hispanic Folklore of Emporia, Kansas." *Kansas Quarterly*, vol. 25, no. 2, 1993.

Sadler, Mrs. James. "The Story of Lady Maud." *Our Young People. Published for the Benefit of the Deaf-Mutes, at St. Francis, Wis.* (November 1911), 144.

CHAPTER FIVE: A TREASURE TROVE OF GHOSTLY GUARDIANS

"FOLK-LORE: EX-SLAVES," *Federal Writers' Project: Slave Narrative Project, vol. 14, South Carolina, Part 2, Eddington-Hunter* (1936): 97–99. Manuscript/Mixed Material. See www.loc.gov/item/mesn142.

Temple, J. H. and George Sheldon. *A History of the Town of Northfield, Massachusetts, for 150 Years, With an Account of the Territory by the Squakheags; and with Family Genealogies.* Albany: Joel Munsell, 1875,18. See archive.org/stream/historyoftownofn00temp#page/18/mode/1up /search/kidd.

CHAPTER SIX: FLYERS, FOLLIES, WHISTLERS, DOLLIES, AND A MEDIUM

Aykroyd, Peter. A History of Ghosts: *The True Story of Séances, Mediums, Ghosts, and Ghostbusters.* New York: Rodale, 2009.

Fuller, John G. *The Ghost of Flight 401.* New York: G. P. Putnam's Sons, 1976.

"Twenty Years After," *Science First Hand.* See scfh.ru/en/papers/twenty-years -after.

CHAPTER SEVEN: GHOSTS MAKE WAR

Carrington, Hereward. *Psychical Phenomena and the War.* New York: American Universities Publishing Co., 1920.

Clowes, Peter. "Angels and Archers at Mons," *Military History,* August 1, 2001, vol. 18, no. 3, 65.

Fassbender, Michael. "The Legend of the Angel of Mons." *Depth and Integration.* See michaeltfassbender.com/nonfiction/the-world-wars /miscellaneous/the-legend-of-the-angel-of-mons.

Miller, Brandon Marie. *Robert E. Lee: The Man, the Soldier, the Myth.* New York: Kane/Calkins Creek, 2019.

Moseley, Sydney A. *The Truth About the Dardanelles.* London: Cassell and Company, Ltd., 1916.

Ruane, Michael E. "Ghosts of the Union's Black Soldiers Rise from Loudoun County's Past," *Washington Post,* March 2, 2013. See www.washingtonpost .com/local/ghosts-of-the-unions-black-soldiers-rise-from-loudoun -countys-past/2013/03/02/2273e41e-7f7c-11e2-8074-b26a871b165a _story.html?utm_term=.ed3d04bac9e9.

CHAPTER 8: GHOSTS RIDE THE RAILS

Berntson, Ben. "Railroad Bill," *Encyclopedia of Alabama*. See www
.encyclopediaofalabama.org/article/h-1258.

Campagna, Phil. "The St. Louis Ghost Train Light ... Explained!" See www
.philcampagna.com/stlouisghostlight/ghost.html.

"Ghost Hunting Groups Becoming Popular," CBS News, May 31,
2008/11:52 PM/AP. See www.cbsnews.com/news/ghost-hunting-groups
-becoming-popular.

Grundhauser, Eric. "The Silver Arrow, the Real Ghost Train Haunting the
Stockholm Metro," *Atlas Obscura*, October 7, 2015. See www.atlasobscura
.com/articles/the-silver-arrow-the-real-ghost-train-haunting-the
-stockholm-metro.

Mathews, Burgin. "Looking for Railroad Bill: On the Trail of an Alabama
Badman," *Southern Cultures*, vol. 9, no. 3 (Fall 2003): 83.

Parcels, Breanne. "UU 'Mythbusters' Investigate Lincoln Train," *Urbana Daily
Citizen*, April 28, 2007.

Selzer, Adam. "Lincoln's Phantom Funeral Train Described in 1872,"
Mysterious Chicago, February 22, 2014, mysteriouschicago.com/lincolns
-phantom-funeral-train-described-in-1872.

Yanko, Dave. "The St. Louis Ghost Train." *Virtual Saskatchewan*. See www
.virtualsk.com/current_issue/ghost_train.html.

CHAPTER 9: HAUNTS IN RED SPACES

Biasco, Paul. "Chicago British Pub Red Lion Prepares to Reopen in Lincoln
Park," *DNA Info*, April 14, 2014. See www.dnainfo.com
/chicago/20140414/lincoln-park/chicago-british-pub-red-lion-prepares
-reopen-lincoln-park.

"Cromwell and the Civil War," *Chavenage House*. See www.chavenage.com
/history.html.

Dubnick, Andrea and John Weagly et al., eds. *Tales from the Red Lion: A
Tribute to the Red Lion Pub*. Chicago: Twilight Tales, Inc., 2007.

"England's Most Famous Ghost at Painswick & Chavenage," Cotswolds.info.
See www.cotswolds.info/strange-things/englands-most-famous-ghost
.shtml.

Murdie, Alan. "The Ghost of Oliver Cromwell (1599–1658)," *EuroParanormal*. See europaranormal.com/ghosts/the-ghost-of-oliver-
cromwell-1599-1658.

CHAPTER 10: GHOSTS SET SAIL

Albert Victor, Duke of Clarence and Avondale, and Prince George of Wales.
The Cruise of Her Majesty's Ship "BACCHANTE" 1879–1882. London:
Macmillan and Co., 1886. See www.google.com/books/edition/The
_Cruise_of_Her_Majesty_s_Ship_Bacchan/LL7o7AF-DIwC?hl=en
&gbpv=0.

"Hair-Raising Canadian Ghost Stories!", *Canada Post*, June 13, 2014. See
www.canadapost.ca/web/en/blogs/consumer/details.page?article=2014
/06/13/5_haunted_canada_sta&cattype=Consumer&cat=mailandmore.

"Phantom Ship Spotted by Visitor," *Truro News*, January 1, 2010, updated
September 30, 2017. See www.trurodaily.com/lifestyles/phantom-ship
-spotted-by-visitor-151203.

CHAPTER 11: HOT SUMMERS, CHILLING GHOSTS

Davisson, Zack. *Yūrei: The Japanese Ghost.* Seattle: Chin Music Press, 2015.

CHAPTER 12: HARROWING CAROLING WITH HOLIDAY HAUNTS

Boniface, Susie. "Kate Middleton Due to Spend a Haunted First Christmas
at Sandringham," *Mirror* (London), December 18, 2011, updated March
15, 2012. See www.mirror.co.uk/news/uk-news/kate-middleton-due-to
-spend-a-haunted-97375.

Collier, Kevin. "After Her Sinking, Especially on Christmas Eve and
Christmas Day," *Grand Haven Tribune*, July 22, 2015.

"English Homes. No. VIII. Sandringham," *Illustrated London News*, vol. XC,
January 1, 1887, 26, books.google.com/books?id=z-9GAQAA "English
Homes. No. VIII. Sandringham," *Illustrated London News*, vol. XC, January
1, 1887, 26, books.google.com/books?id=z-9GAQAAMAAJ&pg=PA26
&dq=sandringham+ghost&hl=en&sa=X&ved=0ahUKEwiUz5HD5qbe
AhUsrYMKHdH0Ca4Q6AEISzAG#v=onepage&q=sandringham%20
ghost&f=true.

Peterson, Margie. "'Tis the Season for Ghost Stories in Bethlehem," *Morning
Call*, December 16, 2015. See www.mcall.com/entertainment/arts-theater
/mc-bethlehem-ghosts-christmas-historic-haunts-20151216-story.html.

Truelove, Sam. "The Queen 'Held Religious Service at Sandringham After
Staff Complained It Was Haunted,'" *Mirror* (London), November 2, 2019.
See www.mirror.co.uk/news/uk-news/queen-held-religious-service
-sandringham-20794380.

ACKNOWLEDGMENTS

I'm "ghost" grateful to my editor, Howard Reeves, who helped me bring these reports to light in ways both creepy and true. I learned *a lot*. And my appreciation goes to Jeff Ourvan, my agent, for leading me to this project.

With thanks to those who spent time helping me channel the vibe and write this book for young readers:

Diana Ross McCain, Zack Davisson, Steve Livengood, Melinda Sedelmeyer, Denise Lundell, Laura German Soeder, Antonia Pigno, Craig Powell, Antonio Garcez, Hank Estrada, Peter Aykroyd, Walter zu Erpen, Pam Senefeld, Tom Hollihan, Johanna Bergström, Adam Selzer, Alan Murdie, Aaron Wolfe, Don Sales, María Cristina Tavera, John Garwell, John Bezosky, Ran Lee, Junghwa Lee, and Duncan Tonatiuh.

PICTURE CREDITS

Page iv: Miriam and Ira D. Wallach Division of Art, Prints and Photographs: Picture Collection, New York Public Library. **Page vii:** Courtesy of the author. **Page ix:** Northwind via AP Images. **Page 3:** From the *Connecticut Quarterly* (Hartford, Connecticut; 1898, vol. 4). **Page 8:** Courtesy of Bee Barnett. **Page 12:** Courtesy of Francis Mariani via Flickr. **Page 14:** Printed with permission of the *Akron Beacon Journal* and Ohio.com. **Page 17:** Courtesy of Aaron Wolfe. **Page 19:** Courtesy of the Cork City Library in County Cork, Ireland. **Page 20:** sixninepixels via Shutterstock. **Page 22:** Mary Evans/Peter Higginbotham Collection. **Pages 27, 33:** Abbie Rowe, National Park Service. Harry S. Truman Library. **Pages 32, 89, 90, 91, 152, 154, 156:** Courtesy of the Library of Congress. **Page 37:** akg-images. **Page 43:** National Railway Museum/Science and Society Picture Library. **Pages 47, 48:** Courtesy of Weird N.J. **Page 49:** Maria Cristina Tavera. **Page 50:** Getty Images. **Pages 54, 55:** Courtesy of State Library Victoria in Melbourne, Australia. **Page 57:** Courtesy of Craig Powell. **Page 61:** Courtesy of Antonio R. Garcez. **Page 66:** From "With the Buccaneers" in *Howard Pyle's Book of Pirates: Fiction, Fact & Fancy Concerning the Buccaneers & Marooners of the Spanish Main* (New York: Harper and Brothers, 1921). **Pages 67, 93, 96, 133:** Getty Images. **Page 74:** Wikimedia Commons/Jon Proctor. **Page 77:** Courtesy of AirNikon Collection, Pima Air and Space Museum in Tucson, Arizona. **Pages 83, 111:** Alamy. **Page 85:** Courtesy of the Peter Aykroyd Family. **Page 99:** Courtesy of the Australian War Memorial in Campbell, Australia. **Pages 105, 169:** Mary Evans Picture Library/Harry Price. **Pages 109, 143:** Courtesy of Canada Post. **Page 115:** Courtesy of Jan Isosaari. **Page 116:** Wikimedia Commons/Maad Dogg 97. **Page 117:** Wikimedia Commons/Holger.Ellgaard. **Page 122:** National Library

INDEX

Note: Page numbers in *italics* refer to illustrations.